Cicero's Cilician Letters

Third Edition

LACTOR Sourcebooks in Ancient History

For more than half a century, *LACTOR Sourcebooks in Ancient History* have been providing for the needs of students at schools and universities who are studying ancient history in English translation. Each volume focuses on a particular period or topic and offers a generous and judicious selection of primary texts in new translations. The texts selected include not only extracts from important literary sources but also numerous inscriptions, coin legends and extracts from legal and other texts, which are not otherwise easy for students to access. Many volumes include annotation as well as a glossary, maps and other relevant illustrations, and sometimes a short Introduction. The volumes are written and reviewed by experienced teachers of ancient history at both schools and universities. The series is now being published in print and digital form by Cambridge University Press, with plans for both new editions and completely new volumes.

Osborne	*The Athenian Empire*
Osborne	*The Old Oligarch*
Cooley	*Cicero's Consulship Campaign*
Grocock	*Inscriptions of Roman Britain*
Osborne	*Athenian Democracy*
Santangelo	*Late Republican Rome, 88-31 BC*
Warmington/Miller	*Inscriptions of the Roman Empire, AD 14-117*
Treggiari	*Cicero's Cilician Letters*
Rathbone/Rathbone	*Literary Sources for Roman Britain*
Sabben-Clare/Warman	*The Culture of Athens*
Stockton	*From the Gracchi to Sulla*
Edmondson	*Dio: the Julio-Claudians*
Brosius	*The Persian Empire from Cyrus II to Artaxerxes I*
Cooley/Wilson	*The Age of Augustus*
Levick	*The High Tide of Empire*
Cooley	*Tiberius to Nero*
Cooley	*The Flavians*
Cooley	*Sparta*

Cicero's Cilician Letters

Third Edition

———

Selected and translated with notes by
SUSAN TREGGIARI
University of Oxford

 **CAMBRIDGE**
UNIVERSITY PRESS

Shaftesbury Road, Cambridge CB2 8EA, United Kingdom

One Liberty Plaza, 20th Floor, New York, NY 10006, USA

477 Williamstown Road, Port Melbourne, VIC 3207, Australia

314–321, 3rd Floor, Plot 3, Splendor Forum, Jasola District Centre, New Delhi – 110025, India

103 Penang Road, #05–06/07, Visioncrest Commercial, Singapore 238467

Cambridge University Press is part of Cambridge University Press & Assessment,
a department of the University of Cambridge.

We share the University's mission to contribute to society through the pursuit of
education, learning and research at the highest international levels of excellence.

www.cambridge.org
Information on this title: www.cambridge.org/9781009383172
DOI: 10.1017/9781009383196

First published 2023

A catalogue record for this publication is available from the British Library.

A Cataloging-in-Publication data record for this book is available from the Library of Congress.

ISBN 978-1-009-38317-2 Paperback

TABLE OF CONTENTS

4

ABBREVIATIONS (*see also Bibliography*, p.50)

AJP	*American Journal of Philology.*
How	W.W. How, *Cicero, Select Letters* (Oxford U.P., 1925)
MRR	T.R.S. Broughton, *Magistrates of the Roman Republic* II, III *Supplement* (Atlanta, Scholars Press, 1986)
SB *A*.	D.R. Shackleton Bailey, *Cicero's Letters to Atticus*, Vol. III (Cambridge U.P., 1968)
SB *F*.	D.R. Shackleton Bailey, *Cicero: Epistulae ad Familiares* Vol. I (Cambridge U.P., 1977)
Stockton	David Stockton, *Thirty-five Letters of Cicero* (Oxford U.P., 1969)
TP	R.Y. Tyrrell and L.C. Purser, *The Correspondence of M. Tullius Cicero arranged according to its chronological order*, Vol. III (Dublin U.P., second edition 1914)

ACKNOWLEDGEMENTS

This selection of Cicero's letters was designed to be used in conjunction with W. K. Lacey and B. W. J. G. Wilson's chapter on "The Provinces in the *Res Publica*" in *Res Publica: Roman Politics and Society according to Cicero*. The more important passages from Cicero's correspondence dealing with his administration of Cilicia in 51–50 BC are translated; brief summaries of some other contemporary letters or parts of letters are included to provide further context. The Latin text followed is generally that of Shackleton Bailey. Those who want full commentary on the texts should consult the standard authorities, in the first instance now Shackleton Bailey and, where appropriate, Stockton's selection.

David Ferrante, then a graduate student at the University of Ottawa, kindly undertook careful checking for the 1972 edition. The strong influence of David Stockton's teaching and published work was the foundation of my interest in these letters. His careful reading of the original typescript saved me from a number of errors and infelicities. The 1972 edition was much indebted to Shackleton Bailey's magisterial *Cicero's Letters to Atticus*. His translation is of unrivalled elegance. I have consulted a number of editors in arriving at my own version: whenever I gave up the attempt to find an alternative word or phrase because I felt my masters had already found the best possible English rendering, I trust I shall be forgiven.

After nearly a quarter of a century, I am grateful that LACT gave me the opportunity to correct faults in the earlier edition and to bring the order and dating of the letters into line with Shackleton Bailey's second great contribution to Ciceronian scholarship, *Cicero: Epistulae ad Familiares*. (His translation of these letters, along with those to his brother Quintus and to Brutus, is currently available from Scholars Press.)

The present revision has new maps and indices and has been entirely reset. Warm thanks are owed for the maps to Sue Rouillard. We were also able to call for help in clarifying Cicero's detour through Laranda and Derbe upon the expert and generous help of Richard Talbert, Director and Editor of the American Philological Association's forthcoming *Atlas of the Greek and Roman World* (expected 1999). My heaviest debt is to the Hon. Publications Secretary of LACT, Malcolm Young, my collaborator and editor. He not only created the indices, but was alert in catching mistakes and quick to solve problems. That the volume looks so attractive and user-friendly is entirely due to him, and to the efficient and helpful co-operation of the printing staff at Cambridge University Press. Any remaining errors are my fault, and I will be grateful if readers will point them out to me.

Undergraduates at Stanford and Yale have kept alive in me the idea that Cicero is not only a uniquely valuable source for his own times but that he is fun. I hope that future users of this volume will agree.

Oxford   S.M.T.
1996

INTRODUCTION

Cicero, who had not wanted a province in 62, after his consulship, was caught out by the legislation of 52 which prescribed a five-year gap between office in Rome and tenure of a provincial command. Ex-magistrates who had never governed a province had to be recruited to supply the resulting temporary shortage of governors. A *senatusconsultum* gave Cicero a one-year term in an enlarged province of Cilicia in Asia Minor. His territory included areas which were normally part of the province of Asia and extended from Pamphylia in the west to the borders of Syria in the east.

Leaving Rome early in May 51, Cicero loitered on the way, with the excuse that he was expecting his legate Pomptinus to catch up with him. He reached Athens on 24 June, left there on 6 July and entered the province of Asia at Ephesus on 22 July, to a warm welcome. Setting out again on 26 July, he finally entered his own province at Laodicea on 31 July, despite the fact that his term was supposed to start on 1 July. This meant that his twelve months would run until 30 July 50. He eventually left the province by the sea route from Tarsus, landed at Side in Pamphylia on 3 August and then sailed to Athens, calling at Rhodes *en route*.

The enlarged province

Phrygia	Assize centres at Laodicea, Apamea and Synnada (part of Cilicia 56–50), (serving Cibyra from Laodicea).
Pamphylia	Assize centre at Side.
Isauria	Assize centre at Philomelium.
Lycaonia	Assize centre at Iconium.
Cilicia Pedias (Lowland Cilicia)	Assize centre at Tarsus.
Cyprus	An assize district by itself.
Cilicia Tracheia (Rough Cilicia)	A military area.

The road runs from Ephesus via Laodicea, Apamea, Synnada, Philomelium, Iconium, Cybistra, to Tarsus.

Cicero's staff

Cicero held the rank of proconsul, and acquired the title of *imperator* as is attested by the correspondence and by coins.

(a) *Legates* (governor's deputies, particularly for military duties):

Marcus Anneius, a man of considerable military experience (*To his friends* 13.57.1).

Gaius Pomptinus, praetor 63, promagistrate (?proconsul) in Transalpine Gaul 62–59, where he suppressed a native uprising.

Lucius Tullius, at some time held a quaestorship; probably no relation to Cicero, since he was recommended by an outsider (Letter 13.5, page 27).

Quintus Tullius Cicero, Marcus' younger brother, aedile 65, praetor 62, proconsul of Asia 61–58, legate to Pompeius 57–56, legate to Caesar in Gaul 54–52.

(b) *Military tribunes*:

Quintus Fufidius
Marcus Scaptius (in Cappadocia, accepted this job but then changed his mind).

(c) *Prefects*:

Decimus Antonius, *praefectus evocatorum* (51).
Quintus ?Paconius Lepta (50), *praefectus fabrum* (in command of engineers).
Quintus Volusius, sent to hold assizes in Cyprus.
Lucius Gavius (51) } given prefectures to attend to business of Brutus
Marcus Scaptius (51) } in Cappadocia.

(d) *Quaestors*:

Lucius Mescinius Rufus
Gaius Coelius Caldus, arrived just before Cicero left in 51, given command of the province until a new governor should arrive.

(e) *Professional Civil Servants (apparitores)*:

Scriba:

Marcus Tullius, mostly working with the quaestor. Though he was closely connected with Cicero (*necessarius*: *To Atticus* 8.11b.4), and a trusted member of the staff (*To Atticus* 8.1.2), we do not know whether his name denotes any other connection.

Accensus (attached to the governor):

Pausanias, freedman of Cicero's friend Lentulus.

There were also minor officials such as lictors, orderlies and criers. Cicero's own personal secretary, Tiro, was with him and gave much help with provincial business. Less important members of his own slave and freedmen staff no doubt filled in when the official civil servants did not suffice. His own entourage included his son and nephew and their tutor Dionysius. Mescinius relied on the help of his cousin Mindius, a banker, in compiling accounts.

The sources on the magistrates among the above staff will be found in T. R. S. Broughton, *Magistrates of the Roman Republic*, vol. 2, under the relevant years. On the civil servants there is a short collection of material in S. Treggiari, *Roman Freedmen during the Late Republic* (O.U.P. 1969), pp.153–159, but note that M. Tullius should probably not be regarded as a freedman of Cicero.

DATE CHART

(Based on Hunter, Shackleton Bailey and Marshall)

51 BC

24 June	Cicero arrives at Athens
6 July	Cicero leaves Athens
22 July	Cicero arrives at Ephesus in the province of Asia
26 July	Cicero leaves Ephesus
27 July	Cicero arrives at Tralles
	(Ephesus to Tralles, 32 Roman miles)
28 July	Cicero leaves Tralles
31 July	Cicero arrives at Laodicea in his province
	(Tralles to Laodicea, 81 Roman miles)
	Assizes
3 August	Cicero leaves Laodicea
5 August	Cicero arrives at Apamea
	(Laodicea to Apamea, 70 Roman miles)
	Assizes
9 August	Cicero leaves Apamea
10 August	Cicero arrives at Synnada
	(Apamea to Synnada, 50 Roman miles)
	Assizes
14 August	Cicero leaves Synnada
16 August	Cicero arrives at Philomelium
	(Synnada to Philomelium, 60 Roman miles)
	Cicero settles mutinous cohorts and sends them to Iconium under Anneius.
	Assizes
20 August	Cicero leaves Philomelium
23 August	Cicero arrives at Iconium town
	(Philomelium to Iconium, 91 Roman miles)
24 August	Cicero leaves Iconium town, arrives at Iconium camp
28 August	Cicero reviews army
1 September	Cicero leaves Iconium town
2 September	Cicero returns to Iconium town (hoping to meet Ap. Claudius)
3 September	Cicero leaves Iconium town for the second time
	(Ap. Claudius had apparently failed to come).
18 September	Cicero arrives at Cybistra
	Cicero meets Ariobarzanes
22 September	Cicero leaves Cybistra
5 October	Cicero arrives at Tarsus
7 October	Cicero leaves Tarsus
	Cicero camps at Mopsuhestia and Epiphanea
12–13 October	Night march

13 October	Cicero saluted as *imperator*
14–18 October	Cicero camps at Altars of Alexander near Issus
21 October	Cicero lays siege to Pindenissum in Amanus mountains (exact site unknown) for eight weeks
17 December	Cicero takes Pindenissum
	Cicero goes to Tarsus and holds assizes.

50 BC

5? January	Cicero leaves Tarsus
11 February	Cicero arrives at Laodicea
13 February –	
14 March	Assizes held in Laodicea for districts of Cibyra and Apamea.
15 March –	
1 May	Assizes held in Laodicea for districts of Synnada, Pamphylia, Lycia and Isauria
Mid-April	Senate votes a *supplicatio* for Cicero's victories.
7 May	Cicero leaves Laodicea for Cilicia
5 June	Cicero arrives at Tarsus
	Because of Parthian threat, moves to the River Pyramus, arriving by 26 June
by 17 July	Cicero arrives at Tarsus
30? July	Cicero takes ship, formally quitting his province
3 August	Cicero arrives at Side in Pamphylia
1 October	Cicero arrives at Athens
2 November	Cicero leaves Patras for Italy

Note:	1 Roman mile = 1.480 km.
	1 English mile = 1.609 km.

CICERO'S CILICIAN LETTERS

1 *To Atticus* **5.15** = SB *A*.108 = TP 207   3 August 51

Laodicea.

1   I reached Laodicea on 31 July. You can start crossing off the days of my
year from there. Nothing could have been more warmly looked forward
to or more welcome than my arrival. But I'm incredibly sick of the whole
business. You'll say "Has your galloping brain, which I know so well, no
room to itself and can your energetic mind find no scope to work?" That's
precisely the trouble. Think of me pronouncing judgement here and A.
Plotius *(sc. the praetor)* doing it in Rome. Imagine our friend *(Pompey)*
having such a huge army and me with two nominal sub-strength legions.
But that's not what I miss: I'm missing you, being in the public eye, the
forum, the city, home. But I'll bear it as well as I can as long as it only
lasts a year. If my term is extended, it is all up with me. But that can easily
be scotched, as long as you're at Rome.

2   Do you want to know what I'm doing here? Running into vast expense
and thoroughly enjoying it. I'm so wonderfully particular about other
people's money, just as you advised me to be, that I'm afraid I shall have
to raise a loan to pay back the bank-draft you gave me. I'm not scratch-
ing the scabs on the wounds Appius dealt the province, but they show up
too clearly to be hidden.

3   At the time of writing on 3 August, I am *en route* from Laodicea to camp
in Lycaonia; then I'm thinking of going to the Taurus to do battle with
Moeragenes to determine who wins your slave. *(A runaway slave of Atticus
had probably taken refuge with the chieftain Moeragenes.)* "Panniers on an
ox, not the right sort of job for me" *(= I'm a square peg in a round hole)*,
but I'll grin and bear it as long as I'm only here a year, *please:* and you
make sure to be there on the dot to wake the whole senate up. I'm very
worried because I haven't heard any home news for so long. So, as I said
in an earlier letter, make sure I hear about public affairs as well as the rest.
I know it will take a long time for you to get this letter, but I am giving
it to a confidential friend, Gaius Andronicus of Puteoli. But you will be
able to send your letters often by the tax company couriers *(Tabellarii
Publicanorum)* and by courtesy of the Rome directors of land tax and
customs dues for my districts.

2 *To Atticus* **5.16** = SB *A*.109 = TP 208   14? August 51

= Stockton 23 = How 29.

On the road between Synnada and Philomelium.

1   Although I am on the road in the middle of my journey and the tax
company couriers are on the point of leaving, I have decided to steal a
moment so that you won't think I've forgotten your instructions. So I've

sat down by the road to write you a summary of things which really call
for a longer and more deliberate exposition.

2   I must tell you that my arrival in this oppressed and almost ruined province
– which took place on 31 July – was eagerly awaited. I spent three days at
Laodicea, three at Apamea and the same at Synnada *(the three chief towns
of the Phrygian districts)*. We have kept hearing the whole time that they
cannot pay the poll-tax that is demanded; that all taxes have been sold[1];
there is weeping and wailing from the communities, and talk of ravages
which sound like the work of a wild beast rather than a human being *(sc.
Appius Claudius)*. To cut a long story short, they are all sick of life.

3   But the unhappy cities are relieved because they don't have to spend
anything on me, my *legati*, my quaestor or anyone else. I must tell you
that I don't even take firewood, let alone hay or the usual perquisites
allowed by the Julian law[2], and except for four couches and a roof above
our heads no one accepts anything; in some places we don't even get a
roof, but stay under canvas. So an amazing number of people are coming
together from the country, the villages, from all the towns; indeed my mere
arrival is bringing them back to life now that they find out the justice, self-
control and mercifulness *(iustitia, abstinentia, clementia)* of your friend
Cicero, which surpass everyone's expectation.

4   When Appius heard I was on the way he dashed off to Tarsus in the
furthest corner of the province. There he is holding an assize. There's no
word about the Parthians but those who come in report that our cavalry
have been knocked about by the orientals. Bibulus hasn't the slightest idea
even now of getting to his province *(Syria)*: they say he wants to arrive
late so that he can leave late. I am going with all speed to the army base[3],
which is two days' march away from here.

3   *To Atticus* 5.17 = SB *A*.110 = TP 209   15? August 51

On the road between Synnada and Philomelium.

1   I have received a bundle of letters from Rome but none from you. Unless
you were ill or out of Rome I think the omission must be Philotimus'[4]
fault, not yours. I'm dictating this as I sit in my carriage on the way to
the camp two days' journey away. Within a few days I have safe couriers
available, so I am saving up till then to write a long letter.

2   I should prefer you to hear this from others, but I can tell you that I am
behaving myself with such self-control *(abstinentia)* that not a single penny
(teruncius or quarter-as) is being spent on anyone. Credit for this is also
due to the carefulness of my legates, military tribunes and prefects, for all
of them are backing me in my quest for glory. Our friend Lepta is marvellous. But I'm in a hurry now. I'll write you a full account in a few days.

[1] See SB *ad loc.* (arguing against T. R. S. Broughton, *AJP* 57 (1936), 174). SB explains that the
cities had had to sell to the *publicani* for ready cash their rights to collect taxes.
[2] An omnibus law of Caesar in 59 *(Lex Julia de rebus repetundis)* restricting exactions by governors
(TP 3, pp. 295–296).
[3] Philomelium, where there were 5 cohorts. The main force was at Iconium.
[4] He acted as Cicero's steward, and forwarding letters was one of his jobs.

3   The younger Deiotarus, who has been given the title of king by the Senate, has taken our boys *(Marcus, Cicero's son, and Quintus, his and Atticus' nephew)* with him to his country. While we are on campaign, we thought that would be the best plan for them.

4   Sestius has written to tell me that he has talked to you about my greatest personal concern[1] and what you thought about it. Please get on with it and write to me what can be done and what you think best.

5   Sestius also writes that Hortensius said something or other about extending my term. He had undertaken at Cumae to insist that I should not be kept here more than a year. (If you care for me at all, make a stand on this point. I can't tell you how I hate being away from you; besides, I hope my justice and self-control *(iustitia, abstinentia)* will shine brighter if I don't stay too long here, as Scaevola found, who governed Asia for only nine months.

6   Our Appius, when he saw I was coming, took himself off from Laodicea all the way to Tarsus where he is holding the assize, despite the fact that I am in the province. I'm not making an issue of this affront, as I have my work cut out healing the wounds which he has dealt the province, which I am trying to do as far as possible without casting aspersions on him. But I'd like you to tell our friend Brutus[2] that he didn't behave prettily in getting as far away as possible when I arrived.

4   *To his friends* 3.6 = SB *F*.69 = TP 213   29 August 51

Camp at Iconium. Cicero to Appius Claudius Pulcher.

1   When I compare my actions with yours, although in safeguarding our friendship I am as concerned for your interests as for my own, I am much more satisfied with my conduct than with yours. At Brundisium I asked Phania *(a freedman of Appius)* – since I thought I had ascertained his loyalty to you and I knew the place he holds in your esteem – what part of the province he thought you would like me to reach first when I took over from you. He replied that you would like me to arrive by sea at Side. So although arrival there would have less *éclat* and was in many ways less convenient for me, I agreed that I would come to Side.

2   Then when I met L. Clodius at Corcyra – a man close to you as well as me – and talked to him, I felt that I was talking to you yourself. I said that I would enter Cilicia first at the place proposed to me by Phania. Then he thanked me but urgently requested me to go straight to Laodicea. He said that you wanted to be on the edge of the province in order to get away as soon as possible, and that in fact if I had not been your successor and you wanted to see me, you would have gone before your successor arrived. This report was consistent with the letter which I had received from you at Rome, from which I could see that you were in a hurry to leave. I told Clodius that I would do this and I was much happier with his plan than with Phania's. So I changed my plan and at once sent you a

[1] Tullia's remarriage.
[2] Appius' son-in-law.

letter in my own hand, which I gather from your letter reached you quite
quickly.

3   I am very pleased with this conduct of mine; indeed I could not have
acted in a friendlier way. Now in turn think about your behaviour. Not
only were you not in the place where you could have seen me at the earli-
est opportunity, but you went off to a spot where I could not have caught
up with you within the thirty days which are, I believe, prescribed by the
Cornelian law *(Sulla's regulation on provincial administration)* as the time
within which you have to leave; the result is that your action seems to
those who do not know our feelings for each other, to be that of a stranger
– to put it mildly – who was avoiding a meeting, while mine appears that
of a devoted friend.

4   Besides, before I reached the province I received a letter from you in
which, although you said you were setting out for Tarsus, you still led me
confidently to expect that we should meet; meanwhile, however, men with
malicious minds – a widespread and common breed – who had yet some
plausible grounds for what they said, not realising my loyalty, tried to turn
me against you. They said you were holding an assize at Tarsus, making
enactments, deciding cases and giving judgement, although you could well
imagine that your successor had taken over. But normally this is not done
even when a governor just knows that his successor *will* soon arrive.

5   I was not upset by this gossip, just the opposite: I thought that if you
were doing anything you were saving me bother and I was delighted that
my one-year term, which I thought so long, had practically been reduced
to eleven months if in my absence one month's work were taken off my
shoulders. But, to tell you the truth, what does upset me is that when there
is such a shortage of troops three full-strength cohorts are missing and I
don't know where they are. I am extremely sorry too that I don't know
where I am to meet you, and that is why I have taken so long to write,
since every day I expected to see you in person. Meanwhile I haven't even
had a letter to tell me what you are doing or where I shall see you. So I
am sending a gallant officer who has my particular esteem, Decimus
Antonius the commander of the time-expired troops *(evocati)*, so that, if
you approve, you can hand over the cohorts to him so that I can get something done while the season is favourable. I had hoped, because of our
friendship and your letter, that I might have the benefit of your advice in
this matter *(sc. the war)*: but I see no hope of that now. But really I cannot
even guess where I may see you, unless you write to me.

6   I will see to it that both impartial and prejudiced people realise that I
am very friendly towards you; you however seem to have given the prejudiced some grounds for holding a different opinion about *your* attitude to
me: if you will correct this I shall be very pleased. So that you can calcu-
late where you can meet me without breaking the Cornelian law, I will
detail my movements: I reached the province on 31 July; I'm marching to
Cilicia through Cappadocia and I'm moving camp from Iconium on 29
August. Now if, after working out dates and routes, you think you should
meet me, you will decide what day and place are most convenient.

5   *To his friends* **8.9** = SB *F*.82 = TP 211   2 September 51

Rome. Caelius to Cicero.

1–2 *(Caelius announces his election to the aedileship.)*

3   In almost all my letters I have mentioned the panthers. It will be a
disgrace to you if you don't do much better than Patiscus *(a businessman
in Cilicia)*, who sent ten to Curio. Curio has given me these very ones and
another ten African ones, in case you think he's only good at giving away
farms. If you remember, you might call up some hunters from Cibyra and
send a letter to Pamphylia – for they say that more panthers are caught
there – and so the thing will be done. I'm particularly keen about this
because I think I shall have to see to everything without the help of my
colleague. So please, *mon général*, make this an order to yourself. You
usually like to be busy while I for the most part prefer not to be. But in
this business all you have to do is speak, that is, give orders and instructions. For as soon as the panthers have been caught you already have men
to feed and transport them, those whom I sent for Sittius'[1] contract. And,
if your letters give me any hope, I think I will send out some more men.

4   I recommend to you M. Feridius, a Roman *eques*, the son of a friend
of mine, a worthy and hard-working young man, who has come to Cilicia
on business: I ask you to treat him as one of your friends. He wants you
to grant him the favour of freeing from tax certain lands of which the cities
hold a usufruct – a thing which you may easily and honourably do[2] and
which will put some grateful and sound men *(the Feridii)* under an obli-
gation to you.

5   *(Caelius concludes with more news of Rome.)*

6   *To his friends* **15.3** = SB *F*.103 = TP 212   3 September 51

Camp at Iconium. Cicero to Cato.

1   *(The Parthians are reported by Antiochus of Commagene to have crossed
the Euphrates and the Armenian king Artavasdes is thought to be about to
attack Cappadocia.)*

2   ... In view of the danger and scale of the war, I am making every effort
to ensure that what we cannot secure by our military resources we shall
hold safe by our gentleness and moderation and the loyalty of our allies
(mansuetudo, continentia, fidelitas) ...

To his friends 15.7–9 and 12 = SB *F*.99–102 = TP 214–217   September 51
*(Between Iconium and Cybistra. Letters of congratulation to the newly elected
consuls for 50, Gaius Marcellus and Lucius Paullus, and to the former's kinsmen.)*

---

[1] Sittius was presumably an agent of Caelius who was interested in a contract or bond (*syngrapha*)
involving provincials. There are other references, equally uninformative.
[2] It appears that these lands, in which Feridius had a financial interest, brought in revenue to certain
(sc. provincial) cities, which held a usufruct (but not ownership) of them. If they were made
immune from tax, Feridius' profits would be larger. The details are unclear, but it is hard to see
how this would have been honourable for Cicero. See SB *F*, Magie II p. 1251 n. 51.

To his friends 8.5 = SB *F*.83 = TP 210   mid-September? 51
*(Rome. Caelius to Cicero: Caelius is worried about Cicero and the Parthian war;
he thinks the appointment of Cicero's successor will be delayed because of oppo-
sition to the supersession of Caesar in Gaul, which will lead to a veto on the
discussion of all provincial terms. For Cicero's reply to Caelius, see Letter no. 10,
page 21.)*

7   *To his friends* 15.1 = SB *F*.104 = TP 221   18? September 51

Borders of Lycaonia and Cappadocia. Cicero to the Magistrates and Senate.

1   If you are in health it is well. I and my army are in health. Although I was
receiving unambiguous reports that the Parthians had crossed the
Euphrates with almost all their forces, still, because I thought that the
proconsul Marcus Bibulus would be able to send you more definite information, I judged it unnecessary to send you an official dispatch on news
referring to a province in another governor's jurisdiction. But now that I
have reliable intelligence on good authority through emissaries, messengers and letters, in view of the importance of the matter, because I have
not yet heard that Bibulus is in Syria and because I more or less share the
direction of this war with Bibulus, I think it right to write you a report on
the intelligence which has reached me.

2   Emissaries from King Antiochus of Commagene were the first to report
to me that large Parthian forces had begun to cross the Euphrates. Since
a number of people thought, when this news was brought, that little faith
could be put in that king, I decided to wait and see if any more definite
news arrived. On 18 September, while I was leading my army into Cilicia
and was in the territory of Lycaonia and Cappadocia, a letter reached me
from Tarcondimŏtus[1], who is thought to be a very faithful ally beyond the
Taurus and a true friend of the Roman people. He reported that Pacorus,
son of King Orodes of Parthia, with a big Parthian cavalry force, had
crossed the Euphrates and encamped at Tyba, and that this had fomented
rebellion in the province of Syria. The same day another letter on the same
subject reached me from Iamblichus *phylarch* of the Arabs[2], who is regarded
as a well-disposed friend to our state.

3   On receiving this news, though I was aware that our allies were far from
whole-hearted and were wavering in expectation of a revolution, I still
hoped that those whom I had already visited and who had experienced my
gentleness and honesty *(mansuetudo, integritas)* had become friendlier to
the Roman people, and that Cilicia also would become more reliable if she
were given a share in my justice *(aequitas)*. For this reason and to demor-
alise those of the Cilician race who had taken up arms, and so that the
enemy should realise that the army of the Roman people, instead of falling
back at the news, was advancing towards him, I started to lead my army
towards the Taurus.

---

[1] A local ruler of part of Mt. Amanus.
[2] *phylarch* = king (roughly). Iamblichus ruled Emesa and Arethusa.

4   But if my authority carries any weight with you, particularly in matters which I can practically see, while you only hear about them, I urgently advise and exhort you to take thought for these provinces, even if belatedly. For you are well aware how I was equipped and what forces I had when you sent me out to what is expected to be so great a war. It was out of a sense of duty and not because I was blinded by stupidity that I undertook the task. For I have never thought any danger alarming enough to make me prefer to disobey you rather than face it.

5   At present the situation is as follows: unless you immediately send to these provinces the size of army you usually send to a major war, we run the risk of losing all those provinces on which the revenue of the Roman people depends. There is no ground for hoping to be able to depend on mobilising the Romans in the province: there are not many of them and those there are run away when danger threatens. That gallant man Marcus Bibulus in Asia has passed judgement on the quality of these troops: although you gave him permission to recruit them he decided not to do so. And allied auxiliaries because of the harshness and oppression of Roman rule are either so weak that they cannot help us much, or so alienated from us that it is apparent that we cannot expect anything from them or place any reliance on them.

6   I think that we may rely on the goodwill of King Deiotarus and on his forces, whatever their strength. Cappadocia is useless. The rest of the kings and despots[1] cannot be relied on either for military support or for loyalty. Despite this shortage of troops my courage and, I hope, my strategy will not fail. The issue is uncertain, but I shall guard my honour and hope also to secure our survival.

8   *To Atticus* 5.18 = SB *A*.111 = TP 218   20 September 51

Camp at Cybistra.

1   How I wish you were at Rome, if it happens that you aren't! For I have no certain information except that I received your letter dated 19 July, in which you wrote that you were going to Epirus round about 1 August. But, whether you are in Rome or Epirus, the Parthians under Pacorus, son of Orodes the Parthian king[2], have crossed the Euphrates with almost all their forces. There has so far been no report that Bibulus is in Syria. Cassius is in the town of Antioch with all his army; I am in Cappadocia near the Taurus with my army, near Cybistra; the enemy is in Cyrrhestica which is the part of Syria nearest my province. I am writing to the Senate about this: if you are at Rome please see whether you think the letter[3] ought to be delivered, and please look after many other things – or rather everything, but especially the vital point, that I'm not given any extra duties or term of office between, as the saying is, the cup and the lip. With my shaky

---

[1] e.g. Brogitaros of Galatia; Attalus of Paphlagonia; Aristarchus of Colchis; Ptolemaeus of Colchis in Mount Libanus; Aretas of Damascus; Abgar of Osrhoene. (TP).

[2] Arsaces III Orodes ruled 57–37 BC.

[3] *To his friends* 15.1 = Letter 7, p. 16.

army and lack of allies, especially of loyal ones, I'm hoping to be rescued by the coming of winter. If winter comes and the Parthians don't get to my province first, then my only fear is that the Senate will refuse to let Pompey leave because of insecurity in the City. But if they send someone else in the spring, I don't care, as long as my command is not prolonged.

2   So this is what I ask you if you are in Rome; if you aren't or even if you are there, I will now tell you how things are going here: our courage is high and we hope – since our strategy is, I think, sound – that we shall hold our own. We are occupying a secure place, with an abundant corn supply, almost in sight of Cilicia, with unimpeded communications if I need to change my position, and a small army but one, I hope, unanimously well-disposed towards me; and it will be twice as numerous when Deiotarus arrives with his whole force. We have allies[1] much more loyal to me than they have been to anyone before: this is because they find my gentleness and self-control *(mansuetudo, abstinentia)* amazing; Roman citizens are being mobilised; corn is being transported from the fields to safe places. If the opportunity arises, we shall defend ourselves in hand-to-hand fighting; if not, by the advantage of the ground.

3   So be of good cheer. I see you and know, just as if you were here with me, that your friendship makes you share my experiences. But, I beg you, if it is at all possible and if my interests are unassailed up to 1 January, to be in Rome in January. I certainly won't suffer any injury if you are there. The consuls are on my side, and so is our friend Furnius the tribune of the *plebs.* But your care, foresight and influence *(gratia)* are vital. Time is of the essence. But it is rude of me to explain to you at length.

4   Our young Cicerones are with Deiotarus, but if necessary they will be taken to Rhodes. If you are in Rome do write to me with your usual regularity; if you are in Epirus, send me anyway one of your couriers so that you can hear what I'm doing and I can hear what you are doing and about to do. I am dealing with Brutus' affairs better than he would himself. I am now bringing my ward Ariobarzanes into court and I am not defending him. They are an awkward lot and have no money. But I will satisfy you, which is more difficult than satisfying Brutus. However, I shall certainly satisfy both of you.[2]

9   *To his friends* **15.2** = SB *F*.105   21 or 22 September 51
= TP 219 = How 31.

Camp at Cybistra. Cicero to the Magistrates and Senate.

1   If you are in health it is well. I and my army are in health. When I reached my province on 31 July – and I could not arrive earlier because of the difficulty of land and sea travel – I thought that my personal responsibility and the national interest above all required that I should attend to the needs of the army and military preparations. After I had succeeded in

[1] SB explains that these are the provincials; "lack of allies" in paragraph 1 refers to allies from outside the province; people like Deiotarus were in short supply.
[2] The Senate had put Ariobarzanes of Cappadocia under Cicero's protection. Brutus was one of his creditors.

making these preparations, thanks to my own carefulness and hard work rather than to any abundance of resources, and oral and written reports of a Parthian invasion of Syria were reaching me almost every day, I decided to march through Lycaonia, Isauria and Cappadocia (*i.e. via Laranda and Derbe*). For there was a strong suspicion that if the Parthians attempted to leave Syria and make an incursion into my province, they would take the most accessible route, via Cappadocia.

2   So I marched my army through the part of Cappadocia which adjoins Cilicia and pitched camp at Cybistra, a town near the Taurus, so that whichever side King Artavasdes of Armenia favoured,[1] he would at least know that an army of the Roman people was not far from his frontier, and so that King Deiotarus, that loyal friend of the Republic, would be in the closest possible contact with me, so that the Republic could benefit from his counsel and resources.

3   While I was encamped in this place and had sent cavalry (*? from Iconium, SB*) into Cilicia so that the announcement of my arrival might encourage the communities there and so that I might have early information about events in Syria, I considered it essential to devote the three days which I spent in the camp to a vitally important piece of work.

4   Since you passed a resolution that I should protect King Ariobarzanes[2] the Pious and the Friend of Rome (*Eusebes and Philorhomaeus*) and defend the safety of the king and the security of his kingdom, and guard the king and his kingdom, and you added that the king's life was a matter of concern to the People and Senate – a decree which has never been paralleled by our order (*the Senate*) for any other monarch – I thought I should report your decision to the king and promise him my protection, loyalty and diligence, so that, since his safety and the security of his kingdom had been entrusted to me by you, he might tell me if he needed anything.

5   When I had spoken of these matters in my council with the king, at the beginning of his speech he very properly thanked you, and then me personally, because it seemed to him a very great honour that the Senate and People of Rome should be so concerned about his safety and that I should show such diligence in making it clear how punctilious I was and how much weight was given to your recommendation of him. And at first in conversation he said, to my great delight, that he had no knowledge or even suspicion of any plots against his life or his kingdom. After congratulating him and telling him I was very pleased, I however warned the young man to remember the mischance of his father's assassination and to protect himself vigilantly and to follow the Senate's advice by taking care of his safety. He then went away to the town of Cybistra.

6   But next day he came to me in the camp with his brother Ariarathes[3] and some of his father's older friends, and, in great distress and in floods

---

[1] He was related both to Orodes and to Deiotarus, so it was hard to guess whether he would join Parthia or Rome.

[2] Had succeeded (*c.* 54) his murdered father Ariobarzanes II as king of Cappadocia and was to reign until 42 BC when Cassius killed him.

[3] Succeeded Ariobarzanes III and reigned 42–41.

of tears (accompanied in this too by his brother and friends) he began to implore me to remember my word and your commission to me. When I asked in surprise what development had taken place, he said that he had received information of manifest plots, which had been concealed until my arrival, because those who were in a position to reveal them had kept quiet out of fear. But at that point, because they hoped I would protect them, many of them had boldly informed him of what they knew. Among them was his devotedly loyal brother, who said, and repeated it in my presence, that overtures had been made asking him to consent to being made king; however this could not happen while his brother was alive. He had been too afraid of the risk of death to disclose this up to that time. When the king had told me all this, I advised him to use all care to protect himself and I urged the trusted friends of his father and grandfather to learn their lesson from the untimely end of his father and to defend their king's life with all care and caution.

7   When the king asked me for cavalry and cohorts from my army, although I realised that by the terms of your resolution I was not just allowed, but bound, to agree, yet since the public security demanded because of the daily reports from Syria that I lead the army as soon as possible to the boundaries of Cilicia, and since now that the plots were unmasked it seemed that the king did not need the army of the Roman people but could defend himself on his own, I urged him to make the preservation of his life his first lesson in kingship. If he discovered anyone plotting against him, he should use the royal prerogative against them; he could punish those who needed it and free the rest from fear. He could use the protection of my army to overawe rather than to coerce the guilty, but since everyone knew about the Senate's resolution, they would realise that if need arose I should protect the king in accordance with your mandate.

8   After encouraging him in this way I moved the army from there and started the journey to Cilicia, leaving Cappadocia with the feeling that thanks to your counsel my arrival had, by an extraordinary and providential chance, freed from the immediate threat of danger a king to whom you had, without being asked, given an honorific title and whom you had entrusted to my protection and whose safety you had resolved was a matter of concern. I think it relevant to report this to you so that you will realise that you long ago took precautions against something which very nearly *did* occur. I am particularly anxious to give you this information because I believe I saw in King Ariobarzanes such symptoms of virtue, talent, loyalty and good will towards you that it will become apparent that your great care and attention to his safety have not been in vain.

To his friends 3.8 = SB F.70 = TP 222   8 October 51
(Mopsuhestia. Cicero to Ap. Claudius Pulcher at Rome. A more conciliatory letter than the last. Cicero defends his policy of stopping delegations going to Rome to eulogise Appius, on the score of economy. He asks Appius to support him in his campaign against the prolongation of his term.)

To his friends 8.8 = SB *F*.84 = TP 223   Early October 51
(*Rome. Caelius to Cicero on developments in Rome.*)

To his friends 2.9 = SB *F*.85 = TP 224   About 8 October 51
(*?From camp in territory of Mopsuhestia. Cicero congratulates Caelius on his election, announced in Letter no. 5 – see page* 15.)

10   *To his friends* **2.10** = SB *F*.86 = TP 225   14 November 51

Camp at Pindenissum. Cicero to Caelius.

1   Marcus Cicero Imperator sends greeting to Marcus Caelius, curule aedile elect. You see how letters aren't getting through to me. Nothing will make me believe that you did not send me one on your election to the aedileship, especially when it was such an important matter and such an occasion for congratulation – about you, because the result was what I hoped for, and about Hillus[1] – you can see I have a lisp – because it was what I didn't expect. But I must tell you that I have had no letter from you since the famous election which put me beside myself with joy: I'm afraid that my letter to you may have been lost too. But I have not sent a single letter home without putting one for you with it, and I love no one more than you. But let us (I can pronounce the letter R now) *return* to *relevancy.*

2   It has fallen out as you hoped it would. For you hoped, you said, that I would have just enough to do to earn myself a laurel crown (*i.e. a triumph*). But you were afraid of the Parthians since you placed no reliance on our troops. This is what happened. When I received news of the Parthian invasion, relying on the broken and mountainous ground, I marched to the Amanus with an army reasonably well strengthened by auxiliary detachments and by a certain prestige attaching to my name among those who had not yet had personal experience of me. There's a lot of talk round here about "Is this the man who saved the City? Whom the Senate ...?" You know the sort of thing. When I reached Amanus, which is split at the watershed between Bibulus and me, our friend Cassius to my great delight had successfully thrown back the enemy from Antioch and Bibulus had taken over the province.

3   Meanwhile with my army I harassed our perennial enemies, the Amanienses. Many were killed or captured, the rest scattered; their fortified posts were seized by surprise attacks and burned down. Because of this genuine victory I was hailed as *imperator* at Issus, the place, as you have often told me, where you know from Clitarchus (*a contemporary of Alexander the Great who wrote a history of his expeditions*) that Darius was defeated by Alexander – and then I took the army away to the most hostile part of Cilicia. There I have for the last 24 days been besieging the strongly fortified town of Pindenissum by means of earthworks, mantlets and towers, and with such force and energy that I will achieve the greatest prestige if only the place is rated a town. If I do take it, then I shall send an official dispatch.

---

[1] He means C. Lucilius Hirrus, tribune 53, an unsuccessful candidate for the aedileship.

4   I am writing this to you for the time being to let you hope that you will
get your wish. But, to come back to the Parthians, the events of this summer
have been pretty lucky, but the prospect for next year is alarming. So, my
dear Rufus, keep alert. For choice, see to it that my successor is appointed,
but if that is too sticky, as you say in your letter and I think myself, then
take the easier alternative and see that my term is not prolonged. As I have
told you before, I look for information on political matters, both present
and, still more, future, from your letters. So please do write to me consci-
entiously about everything.

To his friends 8.10 = SB F.87 = TP 226   17 November 51
*(Rome. Caelius to Cicero. Caelius tells Cicero about the rumours of the Parthian
war and assures him that he will do his best to see a new governor is appointed.)*

To his friends 2.7 = SB F.107 = TP 227   Soon after 17 December 51
*(Camp at Pindenissum. Cicero to Gaius Scribonius Curio. Cicero urges the new
tribune not to allow prorogation.)*

11   *To Atticus 5.20* = SB *A*.113 = TP 228   19 December 51

Camp at Pindenissum.

1   On the morning of the Saturnalia *(17 December)* the people of Pindenissum
surrendered to me on the fifty-seventh day after the attack was launched.
"Who the devil are those Pindenissitae of yours?" you'll say, "I've never
heard of them." How can I help it? Could I have turned Cilicia into Aetolia
or Macedonia? I can tell you that such deeds could not have been performed
here or with this army of mine. I'll give you the story in a nutshell, as you
gave me permission to do in your last letter.
        You know how I came to Ephesus, since you even congratulated me on
the welcome I had that day, which delighted me more than anything else
ever has. From there, after getting a wonderful welcome in such towns as
existed on my route, I came to Laodicea on 31 July. There I stayed two
days in great state and with polite language took out all the stings of the
previous four years. In the same way I stayed five days at Apamea, three
at Synnada, five at Philomelium and ten at Iconium. Nothing could have
surpassed the impartiality, gentleness and integrity of my judicial decisions
(nihil ea iuris dictione aequabilius, nihil lenius, nihil gravius).

2   From there I joined the army on 24 August. On 28 August I reviewed
the troops at Iconium. From this camp, because of the arrival of bad news
about the Parthians, I set off to Cilicia through that part of Cappadocia
which borders on Cilicia, with the intention of making the Armenian
Artavasdes and the Parthians themselves think they were barred from
Cappadocia. When I had been encamped for five days at Cybistra in
Cappadocia, I received intelligence that the Parthians were a long way from
that route into Cappadocia and instead were threatening Cilicia. So I at
once marched into Cilicia via the passes of the Taurus.

3   I reached Tarsus on 5 October. From there I went to the Amanus, the
watershed dividing Syria from Cilicia, a mountain which was full of our

perennial enemies. Here on 13 October we killed a large number of the enemy. Pomptinus attacking at night and I in the morning, we captured some well-fortified strongpoints and burned them down. I was hailed as *imperator*. For a few days we used the same camp near Issus which in the campaign against Darius had been used by Alexander, a general who was quite a bit better than you or I. After spending five days there and plundering and devastating the Amanus, we went away. You know there are such things as "panic" and "psychological effect". The news of my arrival put fresh heart into Cassius, who was penned up in Antioch, and alarmed the Parthians. They therefore fell back from the town. Cassius pursued them and scored a success. In the flight their influential general Osaces received a wound of which he died a few days later. My name is popular in Syria.

4   In the meantime, Bibulus arrived. I suppose he wanted to rival me in achieving this empty title of *imperator*. He started to look for his crown of bay-leaves in the very same wedding cake[1]. But he lost his entire first cohort and a senior centurion *(centurio primi pili)*, an officer among the most distinguished in that rank, Asinius Dento, and all the other centurions of the same cohort, and the military tribune Sextus Lucilius, son of a rich and distinguished man, Titus Gavius Caepio. In fact he received a very annoying and inopportune setback.

5   I'm at Pindenissum, a very well fortified town of the Free Cilicians, which has been at war as long as people remember. They are wild men and fierce fighters and well prepared with everything for defending themselves. We ringed them round with a ditch and rampart, a huge earthwork, mantlets, a very tall tower, a large force of catapults and a lot of archers. With great toil and exertion and many wounded, though no damage to the army as a whole, we pulled the thing off. Our Saturnalia was a merry one, for the troops as well, since I gave them all the booty except the prisoners: the latter are being sold on the third day of the Saturnalia *(19 December)* as I write this: the takings amount to 120,000 sesterces. I am giving the army to my brother Quintus to take from here to winter quarters in an area which has not been thoroughly subdued, while I myself go back to Laodicea.

6   That is what has happened so far. But to go back to earlier events. As for the point which you keep making to me, which is more important than anything, the thing which really worries you, that I should satisfy even my Ligurian tease *(probably Aelius Ligus, an enemy and critic)*, I swear nothing could be more fastidious than my administration. I can't call it continence *(continentia)* since that is a virtue which resists pleasure. In all my life I have never been given so much pleasure by anything as by this incorruptibility *(integritas)*. Nor is it my fame *(fama)*, which is very great, so much as the thing itself which delights me. What more do you want to hear? It was worth it: I didn't know myself or what heights I could achieve in this line. I am absolutely thrilled with myself. Nothing could be more

[1] A Roman wedding cake was cooked on bay leaves. Cicero means that Bibulus would not have to look very far for his "crown".

splendid. Meanwhile here's a coup for me: it's thanks to me that Ariobarzanes is alive and on his throne. In my progress through the province I saved king and kingdom by my advice and authority and by making myself unapproachable and not just unbribable to the plotters. Meanwhile I haven't taken a straw from Cappadocia. I have encouraged the downcast Brutus *(to whom Ariobarzanes was in debt)* as much as I could, a man whom I love as much as you do – I almost wrote "as much as you". And I still hope that the province in my year of office will not have to pay a penny in expenses.

7   That is all my news. I'm preparing at the moment to send an official dispatch to Rome. It will be more detailed than if I had sent it from the Amanus. But to think that you won't be at Rome! Still, the result of 1 March is the vital thing. I'm afraid that when the province is discussed, if Caesar opposes his supersession, I shall be kept on here. But if you were there, I should fear nothing.

8–10   *(Roman and private matters.)*

12   *To his friends* 15.4 = SB *F*.110 = TP 238   Late December 51

Tarsus (?). Cicero to Cato.

Marcus Cicero *imperator* greets Marcus Cato.

1   Because of your great prestige *(auctoritas)* and my unchanging opinion of your outstanding moral stature *(virtus)*, I think it of vital importance to me that you should know about my actions and that you should be aware of the justice and continence *(aequitas, continentia)* with which I am protecting our allies and administering the province. For when you know these things, I think it will be easier for me to secure your approval for what I want.

2   When I reached my province on 31 July and decided to join my army with all speed because of the time of year, I spent two days at Laodicea, then four at Apamea, three at Synnada, and three again at Philomelium. There were great gatherings of people at these towns and I relieved many communities of savage imposts and cruel usury and fraudulent debts. Since before my arrival the army had been split up by some mutiny and five cohorts had taken up a position outside Philomelium without a general, without a military tribune, without even a centurion, while the rest of the army was in Lycaonia, I ordered my legate Marcus Anneius to take those five cohorts to the rest of the army, unite both groups in one place and make camp at Iconium in Lycaonia.

3   He carried out his orders efficiently; I reached the camp on 24 August, having in the meantime raised in accordance with the senatorial decree a strong band of time-expired men and a reasonably reliable force of cavalry and volunteer auxiliaries from the free peoples and the allied kings. Meanwhile when after reviewing the troops I had begun to march to Cilicia on 1 September *(the mss. reading, supported by Hunter)*, emissaries sent by the king of Commagene brought me an excited but accurate report that the Parthians had crossed into Syria.

4   When I heard this I was seriously worried about my own province as well as Syria, and in fact about the rest of Asia. So I thought it advisable to lead my army through that part of Cappadocia which borders on Cilicia. For if I had descended into Cilicia, I would indeed have been easily able to hold Cilicia itself because of Mount Amanus – for there are two passes into Cilicia from Syria, both of which are narrow enough to be blocked by small garrisons, and in fact nothing could be more easily defensible than Cilicia on the Syrian side – but I was anxious about Cappadocia, which is exposed on the Syrian side and which has neighbouring kings who do not have the courage to be open enemies of Parthia even if they are secretly friendly to us. So I established a camp in the furthest part of Cappadocia, not far from the Taurus, at the town of Cybistra, so that I might watch over Cilicia and, by securing Cappadocia, put a check to revolutionary ideas among its neighbours.

5   Meanwhile in this crisis and when a major war was expected, King Deiotarus, who had with justification received great honour from you and me and the Senate, a man of outstanding good will and loyalty to the Roman people and also of remarkably high courage and sage counsel, sent emissaries to tell me that he and his whole army would come to my camp. Impressed by his energetic and co-operative action I wrote to thank him and urge him to hasten his arrival.

6   After I had stayed five days at Cybistra in accordance with my plan of campaign, I rescued King Ariobarzanes, whose safety had on your motion been entrusted to my charge by the Senate, from immediate danger of assassination. Not only did I save him but I saw to it that he should rule unchallenged. I restored to a position of prestige and influence with the king both Metra and the man you had warmly recommended to me, Athenaeus, who had been exiled by the savage hostility of Athenais[1]. And since a serious war would have been fomented in Cappadocia if the priest of Comana, as he was expected to, defended himself by force of arms, since he was a young man equipped with both cavalry and infantry and cash, [? without damage from the would-be revolutionaries][2] I brought it about that he left the kingdom and that Ariobarzanes, without any rebellion or military conflict, should hold his kingdom with dignity, the overriding authority of the court being thus established.

7   Meanwhile messengers and letters from many sources informed me that great forces of Parthians and Arabs had approached the town of Antioch and that a strong body of their cavalry which had crossed into Cilicia had been decisively crushed by my cavalry squadrons and my bodyguard which was garrisoning Epiphanea. So when I saw that the Parthian army had been repulsed from Cappadocia and was not far from the Cilician frontier, I led my army by forced marches to the Amanus. When I got there, I heard that the enemy had fallen back from Antioch and that Bibulus was there. Deiotarus was now coming rapidly to join me with a large and strong

---

[1] The Queen Mother.
[2] Text doubtful.

force of cavalry and infantry and with his whole army, but I informed him that there was no reason why he should be away from his kingdom. I told him that if any developments took place I would immediately send letters and messengers to him.

8   Since I had gone there with the idea of reinforcing either province, as necessary, I now put into effect a policy which I had already decided was to the advantage of both provinces, the pacification of the Amanus and the removal of an obstinate enemy from that mountain. After pretending to go away from the mountain on the way to other parts of Cilicia and after actually going one day's march away and pitching camp at Epiphanea, I marched back by night with my army lightly equipped, starting out on 12 October so as to climb Amanus at first light the next day. I broke up my cohorts and auxiliaries into separate attacking parties, one under my legate and brother, Quintus, and myself, one under the legate Gaius Pomptinus, and a third under the legates Marcus Anneius and Lucius Tullius. We attacked most of them before they were aware of us. Cut off

9   from flight, they were killed or made prisoner. We took Erana, the capital of the Amanus and more like a city than a village, and also Sepyra and Commoris *(these three sites are uncertain)*, despite their fierce and long-drawn-out resistance, for they fought Pomptinus, who held that area of the Amanus, from dawn until the tenth hour. We killed a large number of the enemy and after storming the forts we burnt them.

        After these successes I was encamped for four days on the spurs of the Amanus at Arae Alexandri and spent the whole time mopping up the rest of the Amanus and laying waste the agricultural land in that part of the mountain which belongs to my province.

10   After completing these operations I took my army to Pindenissum, the town of the Free Cilicians, which is in a high and defensible situation and inhabited by people who have never been subject even to kings. Since they were harbouring runaways and eagerly awaiting the arrival of the Parthians, I thought it advisable for our imperial prestige to subdue their impertinence, so that the spirits of others who are hostile to our empire should be crushed. I surrounded them by a ditch and rampart, blockaded them by six forts and a large camp, assaulted them with an earthwork, mantlets and towers and by bringing into play large numbers of siege-engines and archers and a good deal of personal industry, I completed the operation on the fifty-seventh day, without any inconvenience or expense to our allies. All quarters of the city were demolished or burnt down and they were compelled to yield to me. Their neighbours the Tebarani were equally malignant and rebellious but after taking Pindenissum I took hostages from them. I then sent my army away into winter quarters, my brother Quintus being in charge of the job of billeting it on newly-captured or recalcitrant villages.

11   Now I want you to be sure that, if these matters come up before the Senate, I shall consider that you have done me a high honour if you pronounce in favour of conferring a distinction on me. *(Cicero means a thanksgiving for the military successes just described. He goes on to give*

*tactful and elaborate arguments in support of his request. The following
extract contains interesting hints:)*

15   But I am talking too much of myself, which is unnecessary when I am
talking to you, the only man who hears the grievances of all the allies. For
you will be informed by the provincials who feel themselves restored to
life by my administration, since they will all with one accord tell you exactly
what I would most wish for; particularly your two great *clientelae* of Cyprus
and the kingdom of Cappadocia will talk to you about me, and also, I
think, King Deiotarus, who is especially closely bound to you. ...

At the end of 51 or in early 50 Cicero also wrote to the two consuls of 50,
Gaius Claudius Marcellus (*To his friends* 15.10 = SB *F*.108 = TP 239) and
Lucius Aemilius Paullus (*To his friends* 15.13 = SB *F*.109 = TP 240), asking
them to support a thanksgiving *(supplicatio)*. A number of routine letters of
recommendation also fall within the winter months.

Soon after 11 February, Cicero wrote to Appius Claudius Pulcher complain-
ing sharply of Appius' misinterpretation of his actions (in letters he had sent
before leaving Asia in 51), protesting that he had made every effort to meet
Appius at Iconium and that it was not his fault they had missed each other, and
protesting his good will (*To his friends* 3.7 = SB *F*.71 = TP 244). Soon after,
a polite and conciliatory letter from Appius reached him. Shortly after 20
February, Cicero replied in a similar vein, stressing the support he had given
Appius, which Appius' friends in Rome must have attested when he returned,
thanking him for a promise of support in return, expressing the hope that Appius
would get a triumph and asking him to support the thanksgiving for Cicero's
victories (*To his friends* 3.9 = SB *F*.72 = TP 249).

13   *To Atticus* 5.21 = SB *A*.114 = TP 250 = How 35   13 February 50

Laodicea.

2   *(The Parthians under the son of Orodes are wintering at Cyrrhestica in
Bibulus' province and war is forecast for the spring.)*

5   Your letter had old news apart from one novelty about panthers from
Cibyra. I'm delighted you told Marcus Octavius *(aedile with Caelius, who
hoped that Cicero would supply panthers to him too)* that you thought *not*.
In future, always say no, very definitely, to such improper requests. For I
am pretty firm by myself, but really inspired by your support to outdo
everyone – you'll find this out for yourself – in self-control, justice,
approachability and clemency *(abstinentia, iustitia, facilitas, clementia)*.
You can be sure that the provincials are flabbergasted to see that under
my governorship not a penny is being spent in expenses either on public
purposes or on any of my staff except Lucius Tullius the legate. He is
generally scrupulous *(abstinens)* but he did take the ? ordinary *(text
dubious)* allowance under the Julian Law but only once in a day and not,
as other people usually do, in every village he came to. Apart from him,
no one has done so, but I have to mention this one exception when I say
that not a penny has been claimed. Apart from him, no one has accepted

anything. I owe this blot on my copy-book to our friend Quintus Titinius *(a fellow-senator who presumably had recommended Tullius)*.

6   After the campaign I put my brother Quintus in charge of the winter quarters and Cilicia and sent Quintus Volusius, the son-in-law of your friend Tiberius, a trustworthy man, by which I mean remarkably scrupulous *(abstinens)* to Cyprus, to spend a few days there so that the handful of Roman citizens who are in business there should not say that they are deprived of assizes; for it is illegal to summon Cypriots to a court held outside the island.

7   I set out from Tarsus into Asia *(the districts north of the Taurus at this time annexed to Cicero's province but normally part of the province of Asia)* on 5 January, with a marvellous send-off from the communities of Cilicia and especially the people of Tarsus. But after I had crossed the Taurus my districts *(dioceses)* in Asia awaited me eagerly, for in the six months I have been governor they have not received a single requisitionary letter from me and have had nobody billeted on them. But before my time this initial half-year had been devoted to making money in the following way: the rich cities used to give great sums for the privilege of not having the troops quartered on them for the winter: the Cypriots used to give 200 Attic talents – an island from which during my governorship not a penny (I am speaking the plain truth without exaggeration) will be demanded. They are dumbfounded at these concessions but I allow them to vote me only verbal honours. I forbid them to give me statues, shrines or *quadrigae (statues of himself in a four-horse chariot)* and I do not cause any bother to the cities, but just, perhaps, to you, when I go on and on about this. Stick it out, please. It was you who wanted me to do this.

8   My journey through Asia gave me reason even to be glad that because the harvest had failed there was a famine – the most dreadful disaster possible – in my part of Asia. For wherever I went I was able by sheer authority and persuasion and without any force, legal action or bullying to bring it about that those Greeks and Roman citizens who had hoarded corn promised a great quantity of it to the communities.

9   On the day I write this, 13 February, I have begun to try cases from Cibyra and Apamea, at Laodicea; from 15 March I shall try here cases from Synnada, then Pamphylia – I'll look out for a horn for Phemius[1] – Lycaonia, Isauria; after 13 May I shall go to Cilicia to spend June there, I hope without interruption from the Parthians. If all turns out as I hope, July will be taken up with my return journey back through the province, since it was on 31 July in the consulship of Sulpicius and Marcellus *(51)* that I reached my province. So I ought to leave on 30 July. I shall first ask my brother Quintus to allow himself to be left in charge – a solution which both of us are reluctant to adopt, but the only honourable one, especially as I cannot keep that excellent man Pomptinus even now, because he is

---

[1] Perhaps Pamphylian horns were famous. Phemius will have been a musician, perhaps a servant of Atticus.

drawn back to Rome by Postumius and perhaps by Postumia too *(wife of Sulpicius, a lady of dubious reputation)*.

10   Now you know about my policy. Let me tell you now about Brutus. Your dear Brutus has certain intimate friends whom he strongly recommended to me and who are creditors of the Salaminians of Cyprus: Marcus Scaptius and Publius Matinius. I have not met the latter, but Scaptius visited me in camp. I promised him that I would, for Brutus' sake, see to it that the Salaminians paid him. He thanked me and asked me to make him a prefect. I said that I did not give prefectures to any businessman, as I had explained to you before. I won approval for this rule from Gnaeus Pompeius when he asked me a similar favour, not to mention Torquatus who asked on behalf of your friend Marcus Laenius, and many others. But if it was only to get his bond paid that he wanted the post, I assured him that I would see that he got his due. He thanked me and left. Our friend Appius had given several squadrons of cavalry to this Scaptius to let him put pressure on the people of Salamis and had given him the job of prefect. He harassed the Salaminians. I gave orders for the cavalry to get out of Cyprus. He was annoyed.

11   Well, then, to demonstrate my good faith, when the Salaminians and Scaptius with them came to see me at Tarsus, I told them to pay the money. They said a lot about the bond and the bad treatment they had had from Scaptius. I refused to listen, harangued them and asked them to repay my kindnesses to their city by settling the business; I ended up by threatening to compel them. They made no objection but told me that they were paying from *my* pocket, not theirs, since I had not accepted the sum they normally gave to a governor, so that I was in a sense footing the bill. They were even saving a bit since what they owed Scaptius was slightly less than the propraetor's usual cut. I praised them. "All right" said Scaptius, "but let us add up the amount." Now although in my traditionary edict *(i.e. handed down from his predecessors and adapted where necessary)* I had said that I would allow an interest rate of 12% per year compounded annually, he was asking for 48% according to his bond *(1% and 4% per month respectively)*. "What," I said, "do you expect me to go against my own edict?" But he quoted a senatorial decree *(senatus consultum)* of the consulship of Lentulus and Philippus *(56 BC)* which said "that the governor of Cilicia should give judgement in accordance with that bond".

12   This gave me a jolt at first, for it meant ruin for the town. But I discovered two senatorial decrees of the same year on the same contract. When the Salaminians wanted to take out a loan at Rome they were unable to do so because it was prohibited by the Gabinian Law *(67 or 58 BC)*. But some friends of Brutus, relying on his influence, were willing to lend at 48% if they could get the backing of a senatorial decree. So a decree was passed through Brutus' influence, "that it should not be to the detriment of either the Salaminians or their creditors." They paid over the money. But later it occurred to the usurers that this decree did not help them at all, for the Gabinian Law meant that the contract was not enforceable at

law. Then a senatorial decree was passed which made the contract enforceable at law – the effect this had was to put this contract on exactly the
same footing as all other contracts *(made in a more regular manner and
not contravening the Gabinian Law)* but not more or less privileged than
the rest. When I had put this point to them, Scaptius took me on one side
and said he had nothing to say against me, but that they thought they
owed him 200 talents[1], which he was willing to accept, though the true sum
was rather less. So he asked me to get them to give him 200. "Very well,"
I said. Then I sent Scaptius out of the way and called the Salaminians to
me. "What have you to say?" I said, "how much do you owe?" "106
talents," they replied. Back to Scaptius. He protested noisily. "You'd better
compare amounts," I said. So they sat down and added it up: the amounts
tallied exactly. The Salaminians said they wanted to pay over the money
and urged Scaptius to accept. Scaptius took me aside again and asked me
to leave the matter in the air. I granted this disgraceful request and when
the Greeks protested and demanded permission to deposit the money in a
temple I refused. Everyone who was there shouted that nothing could be
more shocking than Scaptius' refusal to be satisfied with 12% compound
interest; others said nothing could be more stupid; but I thought he was
outrageous rather than stupid, for he was either dissatisfied with legal interest of 12% or he was hoping for 48% illegal interest.

13   I've given you my side of the case. If Brutus does not approve of it, I
don't know why I should like him, but his uncle Cato will certainly approve,
especially as a senatorial decree has just been passed on behalf of creditors
(I think after you left for Epirus) to the effect that the legal rate should be
12% *simple* interest. Knowing your mental arithmetic, I'm sure you will
already have worked out how much difference there is between the two.
Incidentally, Lucius Lucceius son of Marcus in a letter to me complains
that there is a great risk that thanks to these decrees of the Senate matters
will go as far as the abolition of debts. He recalls the damage done when
Gaius Julius *(? Strabo, aedile 90)* allowed a few days' grace in paying debts
– the worst the state ever suffered. But to get back to my subject. Work up
my case against Brutus – if you can call it a case when no honourable arguments can possibly be brought against it, particularly as I have left the
matter and the case entirely undecided. *(Cicero now turns to family matters.)*

14 *To Atticus 6.1* = SB *A*.115 = TP 252   20 February 50

Laodicea.

1   Your letter reached me at Laodicea five days before the feast of Boundaries
(i.e. on 19 February). I was delighted to read one so full of affection, kind-
ness, care and consideration. I will reply to it [?] in detail as you ask and
I will follow your order of topics and not my usual arrangement. You say
that the last letter you have had from me was from Cybistra and sent on
21 September *(Att. 5.18 – see page 17 – and* 19*)* and you want to know

---

[1] 1 Attic talent = 24,000 sesterces.

which of yours have reached me. About all those you mention, except that which you say you gave to the slaves of Lentulus and those sent from Equus Tuticus and Brundisium. So your energy has not gone for nothing as you feared, but has been well invested, if what you aimed at was my delight. For nothing has ever delighted me more.

2   I am very glad that you approve of my self-restraint towards Appius and my obligingness to Brutus. I had thought this might not be the case, for Appius had sent me two or three grumpy letters on his way home because I had revoked some of his decisions. Just as a doctor whose patient is transferred to another doctor is annoyed with his successor if he changes the treatment he himself has prescribed, so Appius who had put the province on a starvation diet, bleeding it and reducing it as much as he could, and who handed it over to me half-dead, is irritated to see it being nursed up by me; but at one moment he is angry and at another he thanks me, since none of my actions has been accompanied by any criticism of him. It is only the difference of my system that offends the man. For what could be a more striking contrast? When he was in command the province was exhausted by losses and expenses, but now I am in charge not a penny has been demanded for public or private expenses. What could I say about his prefects, staff *(comites)* or legates? or about their thefts, outrages and insolence? But now there isn't a single private house administered with more good sense and order and discipline than my entire province. Some of Appius' friends put a preposterous interpretation on this and think that I want to be well spoken of just so that he may be ill spoken of, and that I do right not for my own glory but to cast him in the shade. But if Appius is thanking me, as the letter Brutus sent you says, then I don't mind at all, but all the same in the course of the day, which has not yet dawned as I write this, I intend to rescind many of his inequitable decisions and acts.

3   Now I come to Brutus, whom at your suggestion I took up with enthusiasm, indeed started to love, but pulled myself up for fear of putting you out. You can be sure that the thing I wanted most was to be able to carry out his commissions, and this has been my chief anxiety. He actually gave me a list of commissions, and you had discussed the same matters with me too. I have carried them all out carefully. First of all, I asked Ariobarzanes to give him the talents which he was offering me. *(A number has probably dropped out before "talents". Purser conjectures C = 100 talents = 2,400,000 sesterces.)* As long as the king was with me, the matter went well, but then he began to be dunned by hundreds of Pompey's agents. Pompey is more powerful than all the rest put together because, apart from all the other reasons, he is expected to come here to take charge of the war with Parthia. So he is being paid as follows: every thirty days *(i.e.? every calendar month)* the king pays 33 Attic talents *(792,000 sesterces)* which he takes from the special taxes and which does not even cover the monthly interest. But our friend Gnaeus is taking it with tolerance; he isn't getting his principal but is contenting himself with the interest, and less than the whole interest too. Ariobarzanes is not paying anyone else, and could not possibly do so. He

has no revenue and no regular income. He imposes special taxes just like Appius. They don't even bring in enough for Pompey's interest. The king has two or three very rich friends but they hang on to their cash as much as you or I would. Still, I keep on writing to ask, cajole or upbraid the king.

4   Deiotarus too tells me that he had sent envoys to him about Brutus' business: they brought back the answer that the king hadn't anything. And that's my own opinion: the kingdom is cleaned out and the king a beggar. So I think I shall either have to resign from my position as Ariobarzanes' guardian or, as Scaevola did for Glabrio,[1] refuse to pay interest or let it accumulate(?). I have, as I had promised Brutus through you, given prefectures to Marcus Scaptius *(not the same as the man of the same name operating in Cyprus)* and Lucius Gavius who are Brutus' agents in Cappadocia, since they are not in business in my province. For you remember that my method is that he can have as many prefectures as he likes, as long as none goes to a businessman. So I had given him two others besides, but the men for whom Brutus had requested these prefectures had already left the province.

5   Now let me tell you about the Salaminians, because I see that you are as taken aback as I am. For Brutus had never breathed a word to me that the money involved was his own. Just the opposite, I even have a memorandum from him, which says "The Salaminians owe money to Marcus Scaptius and Publius Matinius, who are friends of mine." He recommends them to me and adds, to spur me on, that he has gone surety for them for a large sum. I had succeeded in persuading the Salaminians to pay at a rate of 12% with the rate calculated from the last renewal and the interest added to the principal annually *(not monthly)*. But Scaptius demanded 48%. I was afraid that even you wouldn't like me any more if I let him get his way. It would have meant going back on my own edict and destroying a city which is under the protection of Cato and Brutus *(Cato, with Brutus as his assistant, having been responsible for the annexation of Cyprus in 58–56)* and which has also received kind treatment from me.

6   At this precise moment Scaptius thrust upon me a letter from Brutus, in which he tells me that it is his own money which is at stake, something he had never told either you or me before, and asks that I give a prefecture to Scaptius. But I had told him through you that I would not make businessmen prefects, and if I had been going to make any exceptions, I certainly shouldn't do so for this man. For he held a prefecture under Appius and even had a squadron of cavalry, with which he shut up the senate in the senate-house at Salamis and besieged them there till five of them starved to death. So the very day I reached my province I was met by Cypriot envoys at Ephesus and I gave immediate orders in writing that the cavalry should leave the island at once. So I think Scaptius has probably written a biased letter to Brutus about me. But this is my attitude: if Brutus thinks I ought to have decided to allow the 48% interest to stand,

---

[1] I.e. a guardian for a young ward, probably Q. Mucius Scaevola the Augur for M'. Acilius Glabrio, his grandson (consul 67).

although I allow only 12% in the province as a whole, and have declared as much in my edict and have got the most die-hard usurers to agree to it; if he grumbles because I have refused to give a prefecture to a businessman, when I would not let Torquatus have one for your friend Laenius or Pompey himself for Sextus Statius, and when both these men accepted my decision; and if he is cross because I pulled the cavalry out, then I shall be sorry he is angry with me, but much sorrier that he is not the man I took him for.

7   Scaptius must at least admit that at the judicial hearing I gave him the chance of recovering all the money due to him under my edict. I will add what I'm afraid you may not approve: the interest ought to stop mounting up – I mean the 12% interest permitted by my edict. For the Salaminians offered to deposit the money in a temple, but I persuaded them not to speak to Scaptius about this. They have forgiven me, but what will happen to them if *(Lucius Aemilius)* Paullus *(consul 50, related by marriage to Brutus)* comes out as governor? But I did this entirely as a favour to Brutus, who has written a very kind letter about me to you, but when he writes to me is in the habit of expressing himself with insolence, arrogance and complete lack of tact. Please will you write to him about this matter, so that I can hear from you how he takes it? I have already written to you in an earlier letter a careful account of this affair, but I wanted you to be quite sure that a remark you made in one of your letters had not slipped my mind, that I should be quite satisfied if the only thing I take away with me from this province is the good will of Brutus. So be it, if that is what you want, as long as I can achieve it without doing anything wrong. So far as my decision goes, Scaptius has been paid *(despite the fact that he had not accepted the payment)*. You yourself shall have the last word as to whether this was right; I will not appeal over your head even to Cato.

8   But don't think that I have forgotten your orders, which are rooted in my heart. It was with tears that you asked me to have a care to my reputation. Is there any letter of yours in which you have not mentioned the subject? So I don't care who may be angry with me; the right is on my side, especially when I have, as it were, given six volumes *(The Republic)* as bail for my good behaviour ...

13   It is true that, as you have been told, Thermus *(the governor of Asia)* and Silius *(Bithynia)* are being praised; they are conducting themselves very honourably. You can add to the list Marcus Nonius *(? Macedonia)*,[1] Bibulus *(Syria)* and, if you like, me. I wish *(Gnaeus Tremellius)* Scrofa *(? Crete & Cyrene)*[2] had more scope. He is a splendid fellow. The rest are strengthening Cato's policy. I am delighted that you are putting my case to Hortensius. Dionysius thinks there is no hope about Amianus *(? Atticus' runaway slave)*. I haven't seen any trace of Terentius. Moeragenes has

---

[1] See further *MRR* III pp. 148–9.
[2] *MRR* III p. 208.

certainly been killed. I have travelled through his territory and there isn't a living creature left. I didn't know this when I talked with your *(? freed-man)* Democritus ...

14   War with Parthia is imminent. Cassius has sent a stupid dispatch, Bibulus' one has not yet arrived, but when it is read out I think the Senate will at last sit up and take notice. I am seriously worried. If it goes as I hope and my term is not prolonged, then I have June and July to fear. Oh well, Bibulus can take it for two months anyway, but what will happen to the man I leave in charge here, particularly if it is my brother? And what will happen to me if I don't leave so early? It's a terrible mess. At least I have made an agreement with Deiotarus that he and all his forces should be in my camp. He has thirty cohorts of 400 men each, armed in the Roman way, and 2000 cavalry. It will be enough to hold out until Pompey comes. He tells me in his letters that he will be handling it. The Parthians are passing the winter in our province of Syria. Orodes is expected to arrive in person. So, you see, it's quite a business.

15   All I've heard about Bibulus' edict is the provision which, as you say, is a severe reflection on the *equites (i.e. a clause disallowing certain prac-tices by the* publicani*)*. I have one to the same effect, but more tactfully phrased, in my edict, taken over from the edict for the province of Asia published by Quintus Mucius Scaevola son of Publius *(proconsul 97 or 94)*. It goes like this, "A contract will be treated as valid except if it is made in such a way that in good faith it should not be upheld." I have followed Scaevola in many of my provisions, including the clause which the Greeks think their guarantee of liberty, that civil cases between Greeks should be tried by their own law. My edict is brief because I made a logical distinction and decided to split up my rulings into two categories. One is especially about the province and includes the finances of the cities, debt, interest rates, contracts and all business affecting the *publicani*; the other half is on matters which cannot conveniently be transacted without an edict, about taking over inheritances, possession of property, selection of receivers, sale of property, matters usually dealt with and litigated in accor-dance with an edict. Everything else in the field of civil law I have left unwritten *(outside the edict)*; I said that in matters which came in this third category I would make my decisions in accordance with the edicts of the Urban and Peregrine Praetors at Rome. I have carried out this promise to everyone's satisfaction. The Greeks are delighted because they have their own people as judges. And mere nobodies those judges are too, you will say. What does it matter? They at least think they have self-government. I suppose our fellow-citizens have worthy judges, people like Turpio the shoe-maker and Vettius the slave-dealer[1].

16   You apparently want to know how I handle the tax-contractors. I cosset them, I defer to them, I praise them eloquently and treat them with respect – *and* I see to it that they don't bother anyone. The most paradoxical thing

[1] On Cicero's edict see A. J. Marshall, *AJP* 85 (1964), 185–191.

is this: even Servilius Isauricus *(proconsul in Cilicia 78–74)* allowed the validity of the interest-rates which they entered on their bonds, but what I do is this: I fix a day for settlement, one which it is not too difficult to meet, and if they pay before that date I say that I will allow them an interest-rate of 12% per year; if they don't pay in time, they have to pay the interest-rate specified on the bond. So the Greeks pay at a fair rate of interest and the *publicani* are very pleased because they have full measure of fair words and frequent invitations from me. So they are all my intimate friends, and each one thinks himself specially favoured. But, "With them you can never..." – you know the rest of the tag. *(We don't, but the quotation must have gone on "you can never be too trusting" or something to that effect. The rest of this "rag-bag" letter, to paraphrase Cicero's own description of it, is not, except for some gossipy items, concerned with his province.)*

To his friends 8.6 = SB *F*.88 = TP 242   February 50
(Caelius to Cicero. 1–4: On politics in Rome, including the prosecution of Appius by Dolabella and Appius' consequent surrender of his hopes for a Triumph, and the news that Bibulus has lost troops in the Amanus. 5 ... "It will ruin your reputation if I don't get any Greek (sc. Cilician) panthers.")

15   *To his friends* **2.11** = SB *F*.90 = TP 255   4 April 50

Laodicea. Cicero to Caelius.

1   Would you ever have believed it possible for me to be at a loss for words, and not just your lofty oratorical words but my own common or garden ones? But the reason I'm at a loss is "that I'm terribly concerned about what's being decided about the provinces." I am dying to get back to the City and my friends, especially you, and I am fed up with my province, whether because it looks as if the glory I have acquired here can hardly be increased, but might be spoiled by some mischance, or because the whole business is beneath my abilities, since I am equipped and accustomed to take on greater assignments in public life, or because a major war is looming up and it will look as if I am running away if I leave on the appointed day.

2   About the panthers: skilled hunters are, on my orders, hard at work looking for them, but they are in remarkably short supply and those there are grumble, I am told, because they are the only creatures in my province for whom traps are laid, and so, it is said, they are moving out of my province into Caria. However, the job is being energetically taken in hand, particularly by Patiscus. Whatever they get will be for you, but I have no idea what there is. I am deeply interested in your aedileship: today's date reminds me of it, since I am writing this actually on the day of the Megalensia. So write me as detailed an account of the whole state of the republic as possible. I find your reports the most reliable.

To his friends 3.10 = SB *F*.73 = TP 261   First half of April 50
(Laodicea. Cicero to Ap. Claudius. Cicero disassociates himself from Appius' prosecutor P. Cornelius Dolabella and denies any plan of a marriage alliance between himself and Dolabella (that is, through Cicero's daughter Tullia)).

To his friends 8.11 = SB *F*.91 = TP 267   Mid-April 50
(*Rome. Caelius to Cicero, congratulating him on the* supplicatio, *thanksgiving for his victory, approved by the Senate. Political news.*)

To his friends 15.5 = SB *F*.111 = TP 266 = How 38 = Stockton 24
                                                                      Late April 50
(*Rome. Cato to Cicero. Cato explains why he did not vote in favour of the* supplicatio, *but congratulates him because the vote was carried. Cicero replied to Cato in late July* (*To his friends* 15.6 = SB *F*.112 = TP 278 = Stockton 25).)

16   *To Atticus* 6.2 = SB *A*.116 = TP 256 = How 36   Late April(?) 50

Laodicea.

1–3 (*In reply to a letter from Atticus delivered by a courier of Brutus, Cicero discussed first family and literary matters.*)

4   I see that you are pleased by my moderation and self-control (*moderatio, continentia*). You would be even more pleased if you were actually here. I have done wonders at the assize which I have been holding at Laodicea for all my districts except Cilicia, from 13 February until 1 May. Many communities have been entirely freed from debt, many have been to a great extent relieved from debt, all by being allowed to use their own laws and courts have obtained self-government and have come back to life. I gave them the opportunity to shake off or lighten the burden of debt in two ways: first of all there have been absolutely no expenses during my governorship, and when I say this I am not exaggerating: I mean none, not a single penny. It is amazing how this has all by itself allowed the communities to get back on their feet.

5   Then there is a second factor: the thefts committed in the cities by the Greeks themselves, by their own magistrates, were fantastic. I personally interrogated those who had held office in the last decade: they admitted it openly. So without being publicly disgraced they took on the job of giving back the money to the cities out of their own resources. The civic bodies in turn without making a fuss about it have paid the tax-companies (*publicani*) not only for this present five-year period, for which they had paid nothing so far, but also the arrears for the previous five years. I am therefore the darling of the tax-collectors. "Grateful types", you will say. I have experienced that in the past. The rest of my administration of justice has been efficient yet merciful and my approachability has been admired. Audiences with me did not have to be arranged with the usual provincial formalities; there was no need to go through a valet (*cubicularius*). I was up and walking around the house before dawn, as I used to do when I was a candidate. These things are liked and thought much of, and no trouble to me because of my old training.

6   On 7 May I intend to leave for Cilicia and after spending June there, (in peace and quiet I hope, but a big war with Parthia is on the horizon!) I hope to set aside July for my return journey. My year's term will end on 30 July. I am optimistic that my time will not be prolonged. I have the

City Gazette *(acta urbana)* up to 7 March and gather from it that thanks to the strong-mindedness of our friend Curio the one matter that will not be discussed is provincial commands. So I hope I shall be seeing you soon.

7   I come now to the subject of your friend – or, as you prefer it, our friend, Brutus. I have done everything which I could manage in my province or try in the kingdom of Cappadocia. I have been pressing King Ariobarzanes every day in every way, by letter I mean, for we were only together for three or four days during the crisis from which I rescued him. But I haven't stopped asking him, in person at that time and since then in frequent letters, and begging him on my account and urging him and exhorting him on his own account. I have got somewhere, but how far I'm not sure, because of the distance between us. As for the Salaminians, on whom I *am* in a position to exercise compulsion, I got them to agree to settle the whole debt with Scaptius, but at 12% per year calculated from the last renewal of the bond, not at simple interest but at compound interest compounded annually. They had the money ready to pay: Scaptius refused. What do you say to that, since you claim Brutus is willing to settle at a loss? "The bond said 48%." Yes, but that was quite impossible for them to pay, and if they could have paid, I still could not have allowed it. I hear that Scaptius is now regretting his refusal. As for his point that the Senate decreed that judgement should be given in accordance with the bond, that was done to cover the illegality of the Salaminians' borrowing money in violation of the Gabinian Law. That law said that no legal action could be taken about money so borrowed; the Senate merely allowed legal action to be taken about this particular bond. The decree therefore put it on exactly the same footing as all other bonds, and nothing more *(i.e. subject to Cicero's ruling that 12% was the maximum interest rate)*.

8   I think I shall be able to prove to Brutus that I have acted correctly in this matter. I am not so sure that I can secure your approval, but I am positive that I can get Cato's. But to come back to you, Atticus, the eulogist of my fastidious honesty. "Have you dared out of your own mouth" (to quote Ennius) to ask me to give Scaptius cavalry so that he can extort the money? If you were here with me, as you write you sometimes long to be, would you allow me to do such a thing even if I wanted to? "Not more than fifty of them" you say. But Spartacus started off with fewer than fifty men. Think how much damage they would do in a defenceless island like Cyprus. "Would do" I said. But I ought to say, "how much damage they did before my arrival". For they kept the senate of Salamis shut up in the senate house so many days that several died of starvation. This was because Scaptius was a prefect under Appius and had squadrons of cavalry from Appius. So will you, whose face I see in my mind's eye whenever I consider some question of duty and honour, will you ask me to make Scaptius a prefect? But I took a decision, that no businessman might be a prefect, and I got Brutus' approval. Should he have squadrons of horse? Why not
9   cohorts of infantry? Scaptius is turning out a spendthrift. "It's what the chief men of Cyprus want," says he. I realised that when they came all the way to Ephesus to see me and in tears informed me of the crimes of the

cavalry and their own sufferings. So I immediately sent a letter ordering the cavalry to leave Cyprus before a certain date, and for that reason as well as others the Salaminians have exalted me to the skies with laudatory decrees. But what does he need cavalry for now? The Salaminians are paying up – unless we want to compel them at swordpoint to pay at 48%. If I did anything of the kind, should I ever dare to read or even handle those books *(the* Republic *which he had just written)* which you praise so much? You have loved Brutus too much in this matter, my dear Atticus, and me, I'm afraid, not enough. But I have written to Brutus telling him that you said this in your letter to me.

10   Now here's the rest of my news. I am doing all I can here for Appius, as far as my honour will allow but with real good will. I do not hate him and I love Brutus *(Appius' son-in-law)*, and Pompey, whom I must say I like more and more every day, is urging me to it. Have you heard that Gaius Coelius Caldus is coming here as quaestor? I don't know what he's like ... I hope to be in Athens in September ...

To his friends 2.13 = SB *F*.93 = TP 257   Early May 50
(Laodicea. Cicero to Caelius. He protests support for Ap. Claudius and details his plans for the summer.)

To his friends 2.18 = SB *F*.115 = TP 258   Early May 50
(Cicero to Quintus Minucius Thermus, propraetor of Asia, from Laodicea. Cicero advises him to put his quaestor in charge of his province when he leaves.)

17   *To Atticus* 6.3 = SB *A*.117= TP 264   End of May or early June 50

En route to Tarsus.

1   Although I have no news which happened after I gave a letter to Philogenes your freedman for delivery to you *(To Atticus* 6.2 = Letter 16, p. 36), still I must write you something since I am sending Philotimus back to Rome, and particularly about the matter which torments me most, not because you can do anything to help. How could you? for the matter is already in hand, and you are far, far away, "and many between are the waves which the South wind rolls over the broad salt sea[1]". The day is coming closer, as you see – I am supposed to leave the province on 30 July – and no successor has been appointed. Whom ought I to leave in charge of the province? Calculation and people's expectation indicate my brother: in the first place, because it is thought to be an honour, so nobody has a better claim, and secondly because he is the only man of praetorian rank I have. Pomptinus has already left me in accordance with agreement: it was on this condition that he came out here. Nobody thinks the quaestor *(Mescinius Rufus)* is
2   up to the job: he is frivolous, licentious and light-fingered. But there are difficulties about my brother: first of all I don't think I can persuade him to do it, because he can't stand the province, and I agree with him that nothing could be a more unpleasant bore. Then what sort of brotherly

[1] Quoted from an unidentified Greek poem.

behaviour would it be on my part, supposing that he did not like to refuse me? Remember that a big war is thought to be on in Syria, it looks like overflowing into this province, there is no protection here, only the ordinary annual subsidy has been voted. Is it an affectionate brother's job to pass this on to Quintus? Is it a thorough governor's job to leave it to a nonentity? So, as you see, I am very worried and at a complete loss for a solution. I could have done without the whole business. How much better your "province", Epirus, is! You can go away when you like, that is, if you haven't already gone, and you can put whomever you like in charge of Thesprotia and Chaonia. I haven't yet met Quintus so as to be able to ask him if he would agree to the idea *if* I decide on it, but if he could, I haven't

3 yet made up my mind what I want. So that's how this matter stands.

As for everything else, so far there's nothing but praise and gratitude worthy of the books which you praise *(The Republic)*. I have rescued the communities, given full measure and running over to the *publicani*, offended nobody by insulting behaviour, offended a very few people by just but stern decisions (but no one enough for him to dare to complain), achieved military successes which deserve a triumph (in regard to which I shall not act graspingly and shall indeed do nothing without your advice). It is the ending which is the trickiest part, handing over a province. But some god will organise that.

4 *(Affairs at Rome)*

5 I nearly forgot to say that I have done all I could for Brutus, as I have said in several previous letters. The Cypriots were ready to count out the cash; but Scaptius was not satisfied with 12% compounded annually. Ariobarzanes is as ready to pay Brutus for my sake as he is ready to pay Pompeius for his own *(Pompey's)* sake. But I can't go bail for him, since he is a very impoverished king and I am so far away from him that I can only exert influence by letters, with which I bombard him continually. To sum up, in proportion to the sums lent, Brutus is being more generously treated than Pompeius. Brutus has been paid about 100 talents this year; Pompeius has been promised 200 in six months. Besides this, I can scarcely tell you how much I have done for Brutus in the matter of Appius. So why should I worry about him? He has friends who are absolute rogues, Matinius and Scaptius. The latter may be annoyed because I did not give him squadrons of horse to harass Cyprus with, as he had done before my time, or because he is not a prefect, a job I have given to no businessman, not even to my friend Gaius Vennonius or your friend Marcus Laenius, because I was keeping to the policy which I told you at Rome I should follow. But what complaint can be brought by a man who refused to take the money when he could have done? As for the other Scaptius[1] who was in Cappadocia, I think I did enough for him. He had received the post of military tribune from me, which I offered him at the written request of Brutus, and then he wrote and said he no longer wanted the job.

[1] Unfortunately the text is uncertain here.

6   There is also a man called Gavius, who, when at Brutus' request I offered
        him a prefecture, said and did a lot of things to insult me. He is one of
        Publius Clodius' curs. When I set out from Apamea he did not see me off,
        nor when later on he came to the camp and subsequently left it did he
        come to say goodbye and ask if I had any commissions for him, and he
        showed himself, for some reason or other, openly unfriendly. If I had
        treated him as one of my prefects, what would you have thought of me?
        As you know, I have never tolerated rudeness from the most powerful
        politicians, so how could I take it from this lackey? But if I conferred upon
        him a position of honour, that would be more than just swallowing an
        insult. Well then, this Gavius when he saw me recently at Apamea as he
        was leaving for Rome, addressed me in a way which I should hardly dare
        use to Culleolus[1] "Where do you want me to apply for my food expenses?"
        I replied more mildly than the bystanders thought proper, that it was not
        my policy to give expense allowances to people whose services I had not
7   used. He went away in a temper. If Brutus is capable of being alienated
        from me by the talk of this ne'er-do-well, you can love him all by your-
        self and I won't compete with you. But I think Brutus will behave as he
        ought; I just wanted to put my side of the case to you and I have also sent
        a detailed account to Brutus himself. I may tell you (since we are alone)
        that Brutus has not sent me a single letter, even recently about Appius, in
        which there was not something bossy and tactless. You are always quoting
        "Granius now respected himself and hated proud despots" *(from the
        satirist Lucilius)*. But Brutus' manner is funny rather than infuriating to
        me. I must say, though, that he doesn't give much thought to what he is
        writing or whom he is writing to.

8–10   *(on private matters)*

To his friends 8.13 = SB *F*.94 = TP 271   Early June 50
(Rome. Caelius to Cicero on Roman politics.)

18 *To Atticus* **6.4** = SB *A*.118 = TP 268   Mid-(?) June 50

On the march from Tarsus to the River Pyramus.

1   I reached Tarsus on 5 June. There I find all sorts of worries: the big war
        in Syria, the terrible brigandage in Cilicia, the difficulty of administering
        the province now that only a few days of my one-year term are left, and
        the most difficult problem of all, that I am bound by a senatorial decree
        to nominate an interim governor. The quaestor Mescinius – we have heard
        nothing at all about the quaestor Coelius – is the worst possible choice.
        The most correct course seems to be to leave Quintus with *imperium*, but
        there are a lot of drawbacks to that: our separation, the risk of war, the
        unreliability of the troops and a hundred other things. What a bore the
        whole thing is! But I shall leave it to chance, since there isn't much scope
        for planning.

---

[1] It is not certain which Culleolus is meant, but he must be someone Cicero despised.

2–3   (*Private affairs*)

19   *To his friends* 2.12 = SB *F.*95 = TP 263   20? June 50

Camp on the Pyramus. Cicero to Caelius.

1   I am worried about affairs in the City ... (*particularly as he has not heard from Caelius recently*).

2   The City, the City, my dear Rufus, stay in it and *live* in its limelight. All foreign travel – as I have judged since I was a boy – is skulking and paltry to men whose work could shine at Rome. Since I know this very well, I wish I had stood by my opinion! I cannot make any comparison between one little walk and chat with you and all the profit I get by governing a province.

3   I hope I have achieved the reputation of an honest man, but I could have got it just the same if I had turned down the province instead of rescuing it. You put to me the hope of a triumph. I would have had a glorious enough triumph, for I would not have been homesick so long for the things I love best. But I shall see you soon, I hope. Please send me a letter up to your own standard, to meet me on the way.

20   *To his friends* 2.19 = SB *F.*116 = TP 262   About 22 June 50

Camp on the Pyramus. Cicero to Gaius Coelius Caldus his quaestor.

1   When I received the news I had hoped for, that you had been assigned to me as quaestor, I hoped to have the greater pleasure from your secondment the longer you were with me in the province. For it seemed to me important that intimate association should consolidate the relationship between us (*necessitudo*[1]) which has been created by the lot. But when no letter reached me about your arrival, either from you or anyone else, I began to be afraid – and am still afraid – that it may happen that I leave the province before you get here. Still, while I was in Cilicia, in the camp, I received a letter from you on 21 June, written with the utmost courtesy, from which it is easy to see your talent and devotion to duty, but you did not mention the date or your whereabouts or tell me when to expect you, nor had the courier been given it straight from you, so he could not tell me when or from where you dispatched it.

2   Despite this uncertainty, I thought it advisable to send my orderlies and lictors to you with a letter. If you receive it in time I shall be much obliged if you will come to me in Cilicia with all speed. For the detailed testimonials I have had of you in letters from your cousin Curius[2] who, as you know, is a close connexion of mine (*maxime necessarius*), and also from your kinsman and my intimate friend (*familiarissimus*), Gaius Vergilius[3] have great influence with me, as the conscientious recommendations of

[1] The relationship between a governor and his quaestor was traditionally close, but, as Coelius had only just been assigned to Cilicia for 50, little time was left for him to work with his superior.
[2] Not securely identified.
[3] Aedile 65; praetor 62.

friends should, but your own letters about your status and your link with me *(dignitas, coniunctio)* have the greatest weight with me. I could not have been assigned anyone else whom I would prefer as quaestor. So whatever honour I can do you, I will do you, so that everyone can tell that I respected your status *(dignitas)* and that of your ancestors.[1] I can achieve this more easily if you join me in Cilicia, which I think will be best for me, for our country, and most of all, for you.

21   *To Atticus* 6.5 = SB *A*.119 = TP 269   26 June 50

Camp on the Pyramus.

1–3   *(Private affairs)*

3 *cont.* Although my year's service is now almost over (I have 33 days left) I am more troubled than ever about the province. War has flared up in Syria and Bibulus despite his private grief *(two of his sons had just been killed)* has taken on the chief responsibility for the conduct of the war. His legates, quaestor and friends have sent letters asking me to come to his support. Although my army is very shaky, except that the auxiliaries are pretty good but consist of Galatians, Pisidians and Lycians, my chief standby, I thought it my duty to keep my forces as close to the enemy as possible as long as the senatorial decree allows me to remain in the province. But what pleased me particularly was that Bibulus himself did not bother me at all: he wrote to me about everything else, but not about military support from me. And so the day of my departure is surreptitiously creeping up on me. When it comes, there is another problem, whom to put in charge, unless the quaestor Caldus arrives. So far we have no certain information about him.

4   *(Personal)*

To his friends 3.11 = SB *F*.74 = TP 265   Late June 50
(Camp on the Pyramus. Cicero to Appius Claudius, congratulating him on his acquittal, etc. Cicero had received letters from Appius at a camp on the River Pyramus, between Adana and Issus.)

22   *To Atticus* 6.7 = SB *A*.120 = TP 270   July 50

Tarsus?

1   *(Personal)*

2   I have ordered the quaestor Mescinius to wait at Laodicea so that when the accounts are made up I can leave them at two towns as the Julian Law lays down. I should like to go to Rhodes for the sake of the boys *(young Marcus and Quintus)*, then to Athens as quickly as possible, even if the Etesian winds are blowing the other way. But I want to get to Rome while the present magistrates are still in office, because I have seen from the vote of a thanksgiving that they are favourable to me. But please send a letter

---

[1] Coelius' grandfather, C. Coelius Caldus, a new man, was consul in 94 BC.

to catch me on the road, if you think that I ought to come more slowly for political reasons ...

To his friends 2.17 = SB *F*.117 = TP 272   About 18 July 50
(Tarsus. Cicero to Gnaeus Sallustius (name doubtful), Bibulus' proquaestor in Syria, mostly on Syrian affairs, but also mentioning how Cicero handled his accounts.)

To his friends 15.11 = SB *F*.118 = TP 274   Late July 50
(Tarsus. Cicero to Gaius Marcellus, the consul, thanking him for favours (the supplicatio*) and praising his conduct.*

23   ***To his friends* 2.15** = SB *F*.96 = TP 273   August 50
Side. Cicero to Caelius. In reply to To his friends *8.11 & 13.*

1–3   *(On home affairs)*

4   As I left the province I put Coelius in charge. "But he's only a boy" you'll say. But he's a quaestor, a young man of noble family, and it's the usual practice; anyway, there was no one who held a higher office for me to put in command. Pomptinus had long since left; I could not get my brother Quintus to consent: and if I had left him in command, prejudiced people would have said that I had not really vacated my governorship at the end of a year in obedience to the senatorial decree, since I had left my second self behind; they might even have added that the Senate wanted people who had never governed provinces before to be governors, while my brother has already governed Asia for three years *(61–58)*. So now I am not worried, but if I had left my brother I should be afraid of everything. And finally, my choice was not so much my own as based on the example of the two most powerful men in Rome, who have bound to their interests all the Cassii and Antonii *(Pompeius had chosen Quintus Cassius and Caesar Marcus Antonius as quaestors without having lots drawn, while Cicero had merely taken the quaestor allotted to him)*, and I did it not because I wanted to win him over but just because I did not want to offend him. So you had better approve of my decision, since it cannot be altered now.

To his friends 3.12 = SB *F*.75 = TP 275   3 or 4 August 50
(Side. Cicero to Appius Claudius. Cicero had now officially left his province, though he made a brief stop at Side in Pamphylia on his way back by sea to Rhodes and Athens. Here he received the news that his daughter was engaged to Appius' former prosecutor Dolabella. He attempts to smooth Appius' ruffled feathers.)

24   ***To Atticus* 6.6** = SB *A*.121 = TP 276   About 3 August 50
Side.

1–2   *(Personal)*

3   I have put Coelius in charge of the province. "But he's only a boy" you'll say, "and perhaps stupid and irresponsible and lacking in self-control."

Quite, but there was no other way. Your letters which reached me a long time ago, in which you said you were reserving judgement about what course I should follow about choosing a deputy, made me think. I realised what were the motives for your hesitation and they were the same as mine. Should I hand the province over to a boy? That would not be in the interest of our country. Then should I put my brother in charge? That would not be in our interest. Apart from my brother there was no one whom I could promote over the head of the quaestor, who was moreover of noble family, without insulting him. Still, as long as the Parthian war appeared to be hanging over us, I intended to leave my brother, or even to stay myself for the sake of the state, even in violation of the senatorial decree; but when by an extraordinary stroke of luck the Parthians withdrew, my hesitation left me. I thought of the gossip there would be: "Aha, so he left his brother. Doesn't that amount to holding a province for more than a year? And what about the Senate's policy of having governors who have never been in charge of a province before? That fellow has already had a three-year term."

4   So these are my motives for public consumption, but to you I can admit another: I should have been in constant anxiety that he might have lost his temper or ridden roughshod over people's feelings or made a careless mistake – such things happen so easily. Then there's his son, how upsetting it would be ... My friends' letters summon me home to a triumph, a thing I feel I must not despise in view of my present rebirth as a politician. So will you please, my dear Atticus, start wanting it too, so that I shan't look such an idiot.

Cicero's next letter, *To his friends* 3.13 = SB *F*.76 = TP 277, to Appius Claudius, is written in August 50 from the province of Asia. He had already almost dismissed Cilicia from his mind, except for the hope of a triumph (e.g. *To Atticus* 6.8 = SB *A*.122 = TP 281).

25   *To Atticus* 7.1.5–6 = SB *A*.124 = TP 284   16 October 50

Athens.

5   *(Cicero dreads getting involved in the debate about Caesar's command.)* You'll laugh at this perhaps: how I wish I were still in my province! But it would have been a good thing, if this is what I have to face. Though it was a miserable time. By the way, I want you to know this: everything that happened at first – which you too extolled to the heavens in your letters

6   – all that was mere veneer. How difficult virtue is! How difficult it is even to pretend to virtue day after day! When I thought it would be right and glorious to leave an expense allowance to Gaius Coelius my quaestor out of the expense budget decreed to me, and to return one million sesterces to the Treasury, my staff howled, thinking the whole amount ought to be shared out amongst them. That would have revealed me as a better friend to the treasuries of the Phrygians and Cilicians than to ours. But they couldn't shift me. My reputation had most weight with me. But I didn't neglect to give every possible honour to everyone. Let this be a salutary digression, as Thucydides says.

See too *To Atticus* 7.3.8 = SB *A*.126 = TP 294.

But one letter at least shows him still finishing off some provincial business months after he left the province:

26 *To his friends* **5.20** = SB *F*.128 = TP 302 *(vol. 4)*   About 5 January 49

Outside Rome. Cicero to his ex-quaestor Mescinius Rufus. The subject of the letter is the financial statements for which Cicero and his quaestor were responsible.

1   *(Cicero could discuss the accounts with Rufus better if his* scriba *M. Tullius were available. He would not have submitted the accounts without going over them previously with Rufus, if the system had not been changed.)*

2   I would have submitted the accounts at the City if the old system were still in force, but since the Julian Law lays down that accounts are to be left in the province and that an exact copy is to be submitted to the Treasury in Rome, I drew up my financial statement in the province. I did not do this in order to force you to make your accounts tally with mine, but I showed you a degree of consideration which I shall never regret, when I gave you the full-time services of my secretary *(scriba)*, of whom I now see you have suspicions[1]. You took on your cousin[2] Marcus Mindius to share the work. The accounts were compiled between you in my absence; all I did was to read them over: in receiving a book of accounts from my secretary I regarded myself as receiving it from your cousin. If this was an honour, I could do you no greater honour, since I trusted you almost more than myself; if it was my duty to see that no account should be submitted in a way which was detrimental to your honour or interest, then there was nobody to whom I could give the job except the man I did give it to. I certainly did what the law stipulated in depositing two copies of the accounts, when they had been examined and made up, in two cities, choosing the two which seemed most suitable for the purpose, Laodicea and Apamea. So on this subject my reply to you is that, although I was for sufficient reasons in a hurry to deposit the accounts, I would certainly have waited for you, did I not consider that the accounts left in the province were as good as submitted to the Treasury; and so ...

3–4   *(Deal with a very complex and uncertain financial matter)*

5   *(Mentions public money deposited by Cicero's order in a temple, which Pompeius had annexed on the outbreak of civil war. There is one other item of considerable interest:)*

9   You must also consider the fact that all the money which came to me without any violation of the law, which amounted to 2,200,000 sesterces and which I deposited in Ephesus with the *publicani (acting as bankers)* has been taken off me by Pompeius[3].

---

[1] The view that M. Tullius was a freedman of Cicero must be abandoned. See SB *A* on 97.1, *F* on 128.2.
[2] Or half-brother (by a different father) or brother who had taken a different name on adoption.
[3] On this money see TP 3 p.xxxvi.

INDEX 1: NAMES OF PERSONS
Listed by *nomen* (or *cognomen* if *nomen* unknown).

INDEX 2: NAMES OF PLACES

(The numbers and letters in brackets indicate the coordinates on the maps on pp. 52 and 53)

BIBLIOGRAPHY

A. Reference

Broughton, T. R. S., *Magistrates of the Roman Republic* II, III *Supplement* (Atlanta, Scholars Press, 1986)

B. Commentaries

How, W. W., *Cicero, Select Letters* (Oxford U. P., 1925)

Shackleton Bailey, D. R., *Cicero's Letters to Atticus* (Cambridge U.P., 1965–1970)

Shackleton Bailey, D. R., *Cicero: Epistulae ad Familiares* (Cambridge U.P., 1977)

Stockton, David, *Thirty-five Letters of Cicero* (Oxford U.P., 1969)

Tyrrell, R. Y., and Purser, L. C., *The Correspondence of M. Tullius Cicero arranged according to its chronological order* (Dublin U.P., 1st. ed. 1890; vol. 1 in 3rd. ed., vols. 2–6 in 2nd. ed. 1904–1933). (Vol. 3 contains the Cilicia letters.)

C. Translations

Cicero, *Letters to Atticus*, tr. D. R. Shackleton Bailey (Penguin Classics, 1978)

Cicero, *Letters to his Friends*, 2 vols., tr. D. R. Shackleton Bailey (Penguin Classics, 1978, or Scholars Press, Atlanta, Georgia, repr. 1989)

Cicero, *Selected Letters*, tr. D. R. Shackleton Bailey (Penguin Classics, 1986)

D. Biographies of Cicero

Shackleton Bailey, D. R., *Cicero* (New York, 1971)

Lacey, W. K., *Cicero and the end of the Roman Republic* (London and Sydney: Hodder & Stoughton, 1978). Chapter 6, "Out of Rome: provincial government and civil war" (96–107) gives a brief general account.

Mitchell, Thomas N., *Cicero. The ascending years* (New Haven: Yale U.P., 1979)

Mitchell, Thomas N., *Cicero. The senior statesman* (New Haven: Yale U.P., 1991). Chapter 5, "Cicero, the provincial governor" (204–231), particularly for Cicero's thinking about imperial expansion and administration.

Rawson, Elizabeth, *Cicero. A portrait* (Ithaca: Cornell U.P., 1975)

Stockton, D. L., *Cicero. A political biography* (Oxford U.P., pb., 1971). Chapter 10, "Cilicia" (227–253) gives a critical analysis of Cicero's administration.

E. Discussion

Hunter, L. W., *Journal of Roman Studies* 3 (1913), "Cicero's journey to his province of Cilicia in 51 BC", pp. 73–97.

Magie, David, *Roman rule in Asia Minor to the end of the third century after Christ* (New York: Arno Press, 1975, reprint of Princeton U.P. edition of 1950)

Marshall, A. J., *American Journal of Philology* 85 (1964), "The Structure of Cicero's edict", pp. 185–191.

Marshall, A. J., *Phoenix* 20 (1966), "Governors on the move", pp. 231–246.

Marshall, A. J., *Aufstieg und Niedergang der römischen Welt* 1.1 (Berlin, 1972, ed. H. Temporini), "The *Lex Pompeia de provinciis* (52 BC) and Cicero's *imperium* in 51–50", pp. 887–921.

Thompson, L. A., *American Journal of Philology* 86 (1965), "Cicero's Succession problem in Cilicia", pp. 375–386.

Treggiari, S., *Roman Freedmen during the Late Republic* (Oxford U.P., 1969)

Tyrrell & Purser, *The Correspondence of M. Tullius Cicero*, vol. 3, Introduction 1.

F. Background

Lacey, W. K., and Wilson, B. W. J. G., *Res Publica: Roman politics and society according to Cicero* (Oxford U.P., 1970; now Duckworth, Bristol Classical Press series)

Richardson, John, *Cambridge Ancient History (2nd. edition), Volume ix* (Cambridge U.P., 1994), "The administration of the empire", pp. 564–598: gives a useful survey of the provincial system, with remarks on Cicero in Cilicia at pp. 596–597.

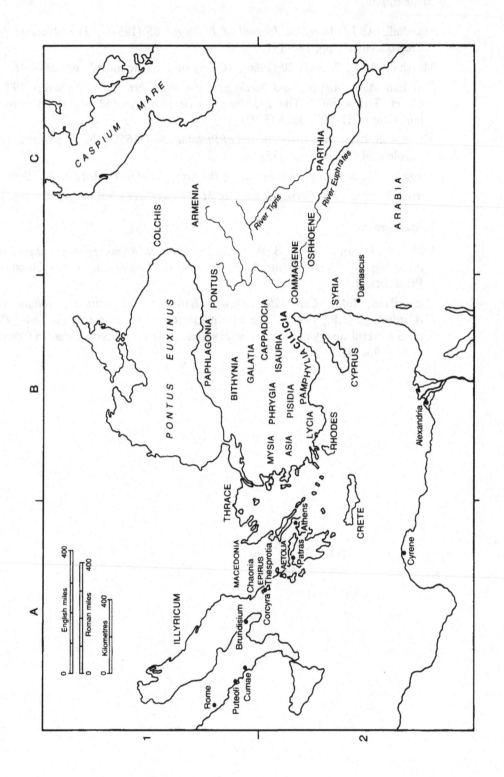

53

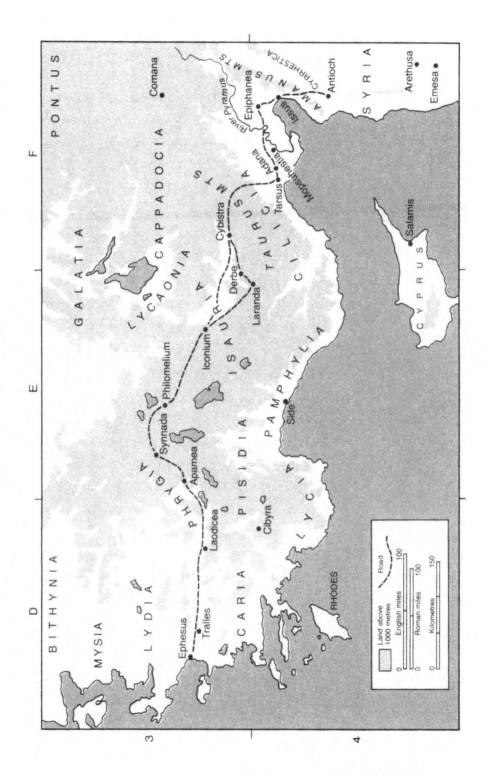

Printed in the United States
by Baker & Taylor Publisher Services

Printed in the United States
by Baker & Taylor Publisher Services